Workshop on Structured and Unstructured Knowledge Integration (SUKI 2022)

Online
14 July 2022

ISBN: 978-1-7138-5642-9

Printed from e-media with permission by:

Curran Associates, Inc.
57 Morehouse Lane
Red Hook, NY 12571

Some format issues inherent in the e-media version may also appear in this print version.

Association for Computational Linguistics
209 N. Eighth Street
Stroudsburg, Pennsylvania 18360

Phone: 1-570-476-8006
Fax: 1-570-476-0860

acl@aclweb.org

Additional copies of this publication are available from:

Curran Associates, Inc.
57 Morehouse Lane
Red Hook, NY 12571 USA
Phone: 845-758-0400
Fax: 845-758-2633
Email: curran@proceedings.com
Web: www.proceedings.com

SUKI 2022

The Workshop on Structured and Unstructured Knowledge Integration (SUKI)

Proceedings of the Workshop

July 14, 2022

Order copies of this and other ACL proceedings from:

Association for Computational Linguistics (ACL)
209 N. Eighth Street
Stroudsburg, PA 18360
USA
Tel: +1-570-476-8006
Fax: +1-570-476-0860
acl@aclweb.org

Organizing Committee

Organizing Committee

Wenhu Chen, Google / University of Waterloo
Xinyun Chen, UC Berkeley
Zhiyu Chen, UCSB
Ziyu Yao, George Mason University
Michihiro Yasunaga, Stanford University
Tao Yu, University of Washington / University of Hong Kong
Rui Zhang, Penn State University

Program Committee

Program Committee

Alon Albalak, University of California, Santa Barbara
Andrew Lyubovsky, Carnegie Mellon University
Ansong Ni, Yale University
Bailin Wang, University of Edinburgh
Ben Bogin, Tel Aviv University
Chen Henry Wu, Carnegie Mellon University
Chia-Hsuan Lee, University of Washington
David Tresner-Kirsch, Brandeis University
Dung Ngoc Thai, University of Massachusetts, Amherst
Enrique Noriega-Atala, University of Arizona
Erica Kido Shimomoto, National Institute of Advanced Industrial Science and Technology
Fahim Faisal, George Mason University
Gyuwan Kim, UC Santa Barbara
Haoyu Dong, Microsoft
Hiroshi Iida, The University of Tokyo
Ishan Jindal, IBM
Jonathan Herzig, Tel Aviv University
Li Dong, Microsoft Research
Linyong Nan, Yale University
Maharshi Gor, University of Maryland, College Park
Michael Saxon, UC Santa Barbara
Naihao Deng, University of Michigan, Ann Arbor
Nan Zhang, Pennsylvania State University
Nitisha Jain, Hasso Plattner Institute
Ori Yoran, Tel Aviv University
Qian Liu, Beihang University
Raj Ratn Pranesh, Pennsylvania State University
Ruiqi Zhong, University of California Berkeley
Saurabh Srivastava, George Mason University
Shiyang Li, UC Santa Barbara
Sheng Zhang, Amazon
Shuaichen Chang, Ohio State University
Shuyan Zhou, Carnegie Mellon University
Siddhartha Datta, University of Oxford
Tianbao Xie, Harbin Institute of Technology
Tianyang Zhao, Pennsylvania State University
Torsten Scholak, University of Toronto
Vardaan Pahuja, Ohio State University
Vasiliki Kougia, Universitat Vienna
Vivek Gupta, University of Utah
Xi Victoria Lin, Facebook
Xi Ye, UT Austin
Xiang Deng, Ohio State University
Xiang Yue, Ohio State University
Xianjun Yang, UC Santa Barbara
Xinlu Zhang, University of California, Santa Barbara

Yilun Zhao, Yale University
Yujie Lu, UC Santa Barbara
Yunxiang Li, The Chinese University of Hong Kong
Zekun Li, University of California, Santa Barbara
Zhen Han, Institut fur Informatik
Zhen Wang, Ohio State University
Zhiruo Wang, Carnegie Mellon University
Zhoujun Cheng, Shanghai Jiaotong University

Table of Contents

Program

Thursday, July 14, 2022

09:00 - 08:45	*Opening Remark*
09:45 - 09:00	*Invited Talk by Heng Ji*
10:30 - 09:45	*Invited Talk by Percy Liang*
11:15 - 10:30	*Invited Talk by Jonathan Berant*
12:00 - 11:15	*Invited Talk by Hanna Hajishirzi*
12:30 - 12:00	*Lunch Break*
13:30 - 12:30	*Poster Session*
14:15 - 13:30	*Invited Talk by William Cohen*
15:00 - 14:15	*Invited Talk by Julian Eisenschlos*
16:00 - 15:00	*Shared Task*
16:45 - 16:00	*Invited Talk by Luna Dong*
17:30 - 16:45	*Contributed Talks*
17:45 - 17:30	*Closing Remark*

FabKG: A Knowledge graph of Manufacturing Science domain utilizing structured and unconventional unstructured knowledge source

Aman Kumar akumar33@ncsu.edu

Akshay G Bharadwaj abharad3@ncsu.edu

Binil Starly bstarly@ncsu.edu

Collin Lynch cflynch@ncsu.edu

Abstract

As the demands for large-scale information processing have grown, knowledge graph-based approaches have gained prominence for representing general and domain knowledge. The development of such general representations is essential, particularly in domains such as manufacturing which intelligent processes and adaptive education can enhance. Despite the continuous accumulation of text in these domains, the lack of structured data has created information extraction and knowledge transfer barriers. In this paper, we report on work towards developing robust knowledge graphs based upon entity and relation data for both commercial and educational uses. To create the FabKG (Manufacturing knowledge graph), we have utilized textbook index words, research paper keywords, FabNER (manufacturing NER), to extract a sub knowledge base contained within Wikidata. Moreover, we propose a novel crowdsourcing method for KG creation by leveraging student notes, which contain invaluable information but are not captured as meaningful information, excluding their use in personal preparation for learning and written exams. We have created a knowledge graph containing 65000+ triples using all data sources. We have also shown the use case of domain-specific question answering and expression/formula-based question answering for educational purposes.

1 Introduction

In recent years, the advancement of artificial intelligence applications has grown multifold. Many areas such as natural language processing, digital twins (Liu et al., 2021), and chatbots (Chen et al., 2021) have become very popular for their ability to record and use information from unstructured sources efficiently. One such application is Knowledge Graph (KG), which has gained popularity in various domains due to its potential applications. A Knowledge Graph is a graph meant to accumulate and impart real-world knowledge, with nodes representing entities of interest and edges representing potentially diverse relations between the entities. A KG has varied applications in recommendations, search, question answering and many more. Most importantly, a KG can be used to make decisions based on inferences.

The use of a knowledge graph is of high value in making design and manufacturing-related decisions. As there has been an explosion of knowledge addition in various design considerations and manufacturing decisions, most of the knowledge is with Small and medium-sized enterprises (SMEs). The decision-making in design and production could be significantly improved using knowledge graphs (Buchgeher et al., 2021). It can benefit not only small and medium manufacturers (Li et al., 2021), but also hardware-based entrepreneurs and help boost self-sustaining product development (Li et al., 2020).

A number of prior researchers have started developing manufacturing related knowledge graphs based on specific problem areas such as machining process planning (Yang et al., 2019; Ye et al., 2018), workshop resource KG (Zhou et al., 2021; Sun and Wang, 2019), intelligent manufacturing (Yan et al., 2020), faults (Liang et al., 2022; Wang and Yang, 2019), maintenance (Hossayni et al., 2020) and industry 4.0 (Garofalo et al., 2018; Bader et al., 2020; Kraft and Eibeck, 2020). However, none of these graphs represent fundamental knowledge of manufacturing concepts, processes, process parameters, characterization, materials, applications, and various other basic aspects of manufacturing domain education. A large amount of such fragmented knowledge can be integrated to assist the learners in intuitively and easily connecting with the knowledge system by leveraging the nodes and relationships. Such knowledge integration will also assist in intelligent question answering that can accelerate knowledge discovery and search.

Google bases part of its Knowledge Vault on the

Proceedings of the Workshop on Structured and Unstructured Knowledge Integration (SUKI), pages 1 - 8
July 14, 2022 ©2022 Association for Computational Linguistics

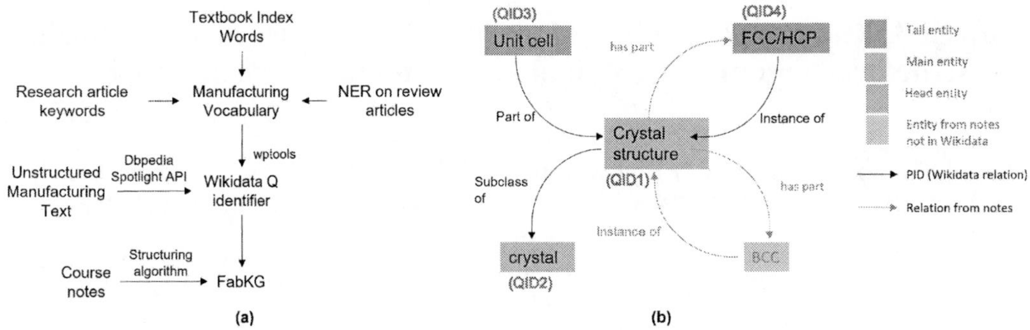

Figure 1: (a) Manufacturing Knowledge Graph construction methodology (b) Use of SPARQLWrapper to fetch Wikidata items associated with 'crystal structure' in two step forward and two step backward. This image also shows addition of entities from student notes.

well-known Wikidata knowledge base (Ringler and Paulheim, 2017). Even though Wikidata has a large amount of information from Wikipedia, there is a dearth of standardized knowledge regarding many important entities related to the Manufacturing domain. For instance, the term 'additive manufacturing' is present as '3d printing'; while there have been substantial developments in the field of 'metal additive manufacturing' (metal AM) over the last decade, it is not present as a subclass of '3d printing' in Wikidata. Moreover, within metal additive manufacturing (Frazier, 2014), sub-classifications such as DMLS, EBAM, and PBF are not present in Wikidata. One reason for this is the volunteer-driven nature of Wikidata as a knowledge base; this has led to a limited amount of specialist terminology and information regarding the manufacturing domain. Therefore, Wikidata cannot provide direct answers to questions that are very specific to this domain. To understand the basic concepts in the context of manufacturing we focus on formulating answers to some basic questions such as, 'What are some precision finishing manufacturing process?', 'What are some tools for machining copper?' etc. The purpose of creating such a knowledge graph of manufacturing using Wikidata is to provide a starting point for a structured manufacturing knowledge base, which can be amalgamated with knowledge from other sources such as textbook (Rahdari et al., 2020) and research articles (Wang et al., 2020b).

To tackle the challenges in developing the knowledge graph from scratch for manufacturing science, we consider various methodologies for creating accurate graphs. We propose a merged knowledge graph that combines the existing structured Wikidata knowledge graph with a novel semi-supervised knowledge graph extracted from textbook data. For extracting graph triples from Wikidata, as mentioned in Figure 1, we have adopted two methods for the approach: (1) Vocabulary-based and (2) Based on Unstructured text. Former includes fetching Wikidata items using a collection of manufacturing vocabulary terms through the utilization of textbook index words, keywords from research papers, and named entity recognition using FabNER (Kumar and Starly, 2021), followed by the use of DBpedia (Mendes et al., 2011) to find Wikidata items. The latter is a semi-supervised approach that utilizes students' notes, considering standard textbooks as the reference. The most significant purpose of the latter method is to make use of textbook knowledge structured by humans, thereby increasing the quality of the knowledge base. The following sections elaborate on the details of the methodology and implementation.

2 Manufacturing Knowledge Graph Construction

2.1 KG construction using Wikidata

Wikidata is a knowledge base maintained collaboratively by the community to represent information in machine readable format. Since no such knowledge base exists for the manufacturing domain, we decided first to extract existing Wikidata knowledge and then merge this with the knowledge contained within manufacturing textbooks.

Wikidata's knowledge graph has Q and P identifiers where Q represents entities, and P represents relations (Hernández et al., 2015). Currently, Wikidata is limited to very few relevant relations between entities for manufacturing domain-specific entities. We have taken about 10 unique relations based on all P identifiers attached with relevant Q identifiers identified by us. The relevant relations in Wikidata include 'Instance of', 'Subclass of', 'Use', 'Color', 'Part of', 'Uses', 'Has quality', 'Has cause', 'Has part', 'Facet of', 'Different from'.

In order to find manufacturing-specific entities in Wikidata, we used the following methods:

2.1.1 Entities extraction from index words of textbooks

Index words located at the end of textbooks are a list of all topics and entities provided to assist readers in finding the location of the text (Kumar and Dinakaran, 2021). These are important terms that are often overlooked but are a good collection of domain-specific entities. We utilized easily accessible 5 diverse ebooks related to manufacturing (Groover, 2020), digital manufacturing (Zhou et al., 2012), manufacturing process (El-Hofy, 2005) welding technology (Kou, 2003) and additive manufacturing (Gibson et al., 2021), and extracted the index entities mentioned at the end of the book to expand the list of relevant entities. We found about 3500 relevant entities from various books and added those to our vocabulary.

2.1.2 Keywords from research papers

We used 500k+ abstracts to create the corpus for manufacturing, as mentioned in FabNER. While extracting the abstracts, we accumulated the keywords mentioned in the abstract, removed duplicates, and normalized many of the words (using Levenshtein distance). There are many words written with some variation in the spelling. E.g., Landau-Ginzburg-Devonshire, Landau-Ginsburg-Devonshire, Landau-Ginsberg-Devonshire, are the same entities with variation in the way it is written in different abstract keywords by various authors. Overall, we found about 4500 relevant entities from a sample of 5000 abstracts.

2.1.3 Named entity recognition on unstructured text

We utilized review articles related to manufacturing to find the most frequent and diverse terms since it generally mention most of the past work and technologies developed in the succinct text. Ten full review articles (Wong and Hernandez, 2012; ElMaraghy et al., 2012; Zhu et al., 2013; Frazier, 2014; Oztemel and Gursev, 2020; Yan et al., 2018; Stuart et al., 2010; Rajurkar et al., 2017; Wang et al., 2020a; Kaur and Singh, 2019) for this part were selected, which were processed using a trained neural network model consisting of BERT (Devlin et al., 2018) and GloVe (Pennington et al., 2014) stacked embeddings through Flair framework (Akbik et al., 2019). Next, we employed BiLSTM and CRF (Consoli and Vieira, 2019) architecture to identify 12 category entities in the review articles with F-score of 83%. Overall, we found about 2000 entities from diverse review articles related to manufacturing.

Table 1: Named entity recognition performance for the Manufacturing dataset

Model	Precision	Recall	F1
BERT+BiLSTM+CRF	0.8185	0.8429	0.8306

Using text and vocabulary of entities from all the above sources, i.e., index words, research paper keywords, and NER on review articles, we further employed two methods for finding existing Wikidata items. As depicted in Fig. 1, in the first method, we used DBpedia spotlight API to find Wikidata items associated with the unstructured text directly based on a 0.5 confidence value. In the second, we provide manufacturing vocabulary terms as the input to wptools python library to fetch Wikidata items as the output. We find all manufacturing relevant Wikidata items to extract a subgraph from Wikidata and later merge this relatively bigger knowledge graph with textbook knowledge (explained in the next section). Upon availability of some Wikidata items, we further used SPARQL-Wrapper (uses Wikidata SPARQL endpoint) and relations list (P identifiers) to fetch forward (head from the primary entity) as well as backward (tail from the primary entity) entities associated with the item. We performed the same for two linked steps forward and two linked steps backward to find most of the nodes that are connected with each other.

2.2 KG construction using Exam cheatsheet/notes for Manufacturing

We propose a novel approach for creating triples utilizing human knowledge. Qualifying exams (or course exams) are part of any doctoral degree program. In some schools, written exams are conducted for a few courses. In some specific courses, cheatsheets/concise notes are allowed for students to bring into the exam to enable the student to remember important points. In most cases, the cheat-

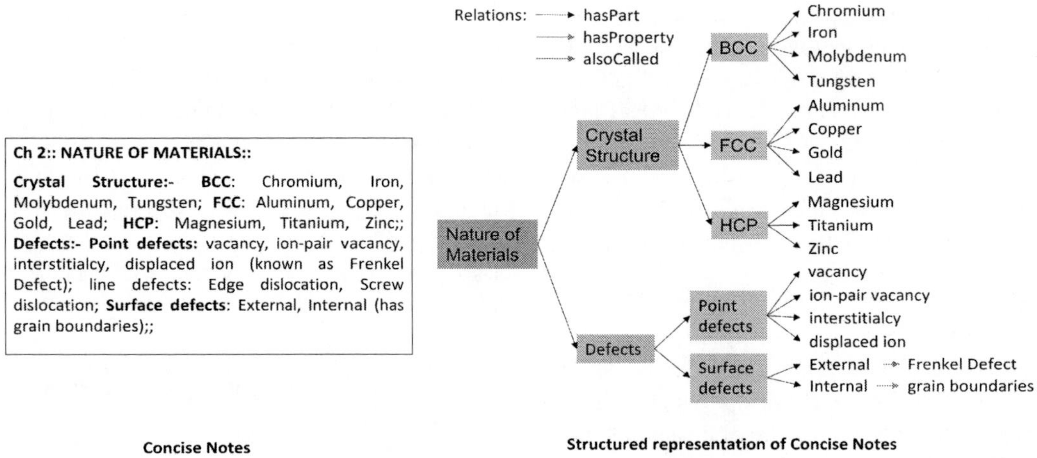

Figure 2: Conversion of concise notes to structured graph

sheet (or notes) developed for the exam are useless when the exams are over. This also means that the verified knowledge written by a student to remember the essential facts is lost or left unutilized for future references.

We devised a strategy for making these short, concise notes be useful input for building connected entities within FabKG. We created optional advice on cheatsheet generation for students to follow prior to the exam at our institution so that they could participate to the task of knowledge base enhancement in the Manufacturing area. Students can only write crucial details from various textbook chapters, assuming that the number of pages allowed in the exam is limited. There is a title within each chapter, followed by several subtitles, each of which contains some entities and context, which is potentially a good knowledge source. The guidelines were kept simple so that students would not have to spend much time referring to them. It mentioned the title, subtitle, and content hierarchy and a precise technique for separating them.

The following guidelines are provided for example purposes only:

a) The chapter name is preserved as the top title, followed by a distinctive symbol, making it easier to distinguish between chapters.

b) Within a chapter, many sub-topics are separated by another unique symbol, such as a double semi-colon ';;'. Two sub-topics are shown in Fig. 2, for example, (1) Defects and (2) Crystal structure

c) If there is a further subtopic within a subtopic, it is separated by a symbol such as ':' followed by some relevant points. A single semi-colon separates multiple subtopics.

d) Explanations or additional information about any term are retained in brackets as an attribute of a relational entity. For example, displaced ion (Frenkel defect) denotes that a point defect with a displaced ion is also known as a Frenkel defect.

Use of some symbols patterns when creating the notes aided in the design of regex patterns for quickly extracting entities and their obvious relationships. We were able to extract over 1200 distinct entities, 25 unique relations, and 4200 unique triples using this method. Fig. 2 depicts the notes in their raw and structured state. The student notes in both unstructured and structured form was verified by human supervision. Indirect crowdsourcing is the crucial aspect that has made this element of the project possible. However, the intention was to use note takers' knowledge. It should be emphasized that even though some previous work has mentioned the use of notes (Denny et al., 2015) for developing a knowledge map, however, on a larger scale and for educational applications, this type of knowledge source has not been studied. This method might be used with little effort for any domain-specific textual material.

Despite the small number of entities/relations discovered, this method allows textbook knowledge to be converted into useable knowledge, which aids in developing a knowledge graph for educational purposes. In general, for automatic extraction of directed relation, it is often difficult to determine which entities are related to each other when more than 2 entities are present in a sentence. This is also because, on multiple occasions, no relation exists between the entities. It becomes a challenge to employ a NER and detect directed relations between entities automatically which we solve by this semi-supervised method. Based on the analysis of the notes, some of the crucial relations found include: 'has', 'hasProperty', 'uses', 'usedTo', 'usedIn', 'causes', 'producedBy', 'makes', 'hasExpression', 'hasPart', 'addedWith', 'hasValue', 'includes', 'partOf', 'alsoCalled', 'dueTo', 'instanceOf', 'isAbbrev', 'isAcronym', 'hasComparator'.

2.3 Fusion of structured and unstructured knowledge

All triples found with the above-mentioned methods were aggregated together to create a knowledge graph of about 65000 triples. Fig1(b) depicts the merger of Wikidata and textbook knowledge. We created a collection of possible synonyms for various entities to enable us to merge Wikidata entities with textbook entities. We found that out of 1200 textbook entities, about 25% were present in Wikidata. We also found some links between entities which otherwise were not present in Wikidata due to limited relations.

3 Knowledge driven QA

3.1 Domain specific question answering

The Knowledge Graph for manufacturing (FabKG) is suitable for answering questions and powering a chatbot to answer questions. The FabKG is a directed graph G = (V, E) where the node $v \in V$ denotes named entities of manufacturing, numeric literal or expression, and the edge $e \in E$ denotes directed relation between the nodes.

Given a natural language question as input, the entities are categorized in their respective classes. Based on the subject and predicate most similar object (highest cosine similarity) to the category in the knowledge base is queried.

Some of the common domain specific questions could not be answered using general purpose search engines. Examples of questions that could be answered by FabKG are:

a. Which tool geometry is used for planning?

b. Which material has more hardness, cermet or alumina? Note: We have used a hasComparator relation specifying various comparison values in our KG that could answer the 'more' and 'less' inference question.

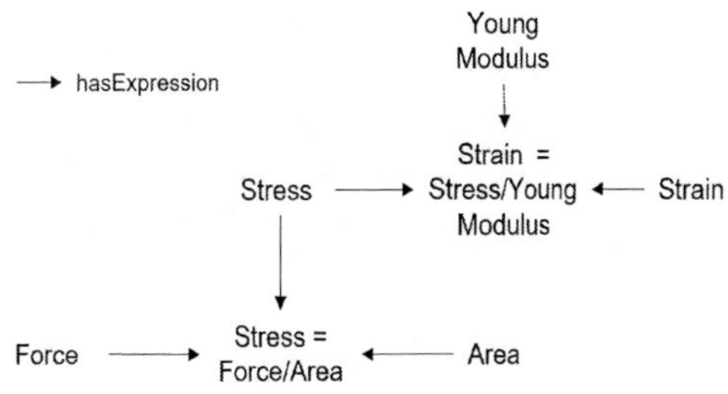

Figure 3: A small subgraph showing the links of entities connected with other expressions for ease of calculation, making the system think like humans.

c. What is the composition of Tungsten in cast cobalt?

d. Which nontraditional manufacturing process is used for coining operations?

e. What is the length to depth ratio for discontinuous fibers?

3.2 Expression based question answering

We have included some manufacturing-specific formulas/expressions in the knowledge graph to enable inference-based calculations. Since we have captured some formulae linked with entities using 'hasExpression' relation, traversing for the formula node in the graph is easy. We have also included a simple rule for calculation-type questions. Here is an example question below:

> Calculate the strain on the cylinder given the area 1 cm^2, 10N force, and Young's modulus for steel 200 GPa.

Given the question above, we have some 'formula entities': area, force, and young modulus of steel. These entities are queried in the KG for any available linked expression. Similar to MathGraph (Zhao et al., 2019), we utilize SymPy (Meurer et al., 2017) to convert the queried expression into a mathematical equation with variables, and to perform the calculation, we use some basic rules of precedence to fetch the results. As shown in fig. 3, we can find strain using Young's modulus and stress; however, since stress is not known, we calculate stress as the first step using force and area. This process depicts the way human thinks while answering a question with some inputs and related expressions.

Some other examples of questions forms that are easier than the above-mentioned questions: a. Calculate material removal rate given feed rate, cutting speed, and depth of cut. HINT: We can calculate the Material removal rate using (feed rate)*(cutting speed)*(depth of cut). b. Calculate measuring length of roughness given cutoff length of 0.8. HINT: measuring length of roughness = 0.5 * cutoff length.

4 Conclusion and future work

We have developed FabKG – a knowledge graph for product design and manufacturing, which utilizes two critical sources of knowledge, (1) Wikidata and (2) Human constructed notes, that combine structured/unstructured knowledge towards answering question-related to product development and manufacturing. Using this KG, students, product developers, and knowledge seekers can get good insights into various concepts and fundamentals about various topics in this domain. Using all the methods described above, we have found 65000+ triples in 12 entity categories.

In the future, we plan to use the heterogeneous knowledge graph for directed relation prediction in the bigger corpus, performing graph embedding and link prediction. Moreover, lecture presentations with succinct text could also be utilized for finding entities and relations. Generally, the title/topic of the presentation symbolizes the subject, with some entities either written directly or placed after another subtopic. Furthermore, 'property/attribute' of relation through the specific value of entities such as the strength of materials, carbon content, Brinell hardness, Etc., currently available in tabular form in books and other resources, can be added to the KG. The same could be represented using a hypergraph by combining multimodal data. Therefore, the new graph structure would have not only an 'entity-relation-entity' type graph but also an 'entity-attribute-value' graph. Finally, this knowledge graph could help link to global knowledge by contributing to existing Wikidata knowledge with the help of Wikimapper.

References

Alan Akbik, Tanja Bergmann, Duncan Blythe, Kashif Rasul, Stefan Schweter, and Roland Vollgraf. 2019. Flair: An easy-to-use framework for state-of-the-art nlp. In *Proceedings of the 2019 Conference of the North American Chapter of the Association for Computational Linguistics (Demonstrations)*, pages 54–59.

Sebastian R Bader, Irlan Grangel-Gonzalez, Priyanka Nanjappa, Maria-Esther Vidal, and Maria Maleshkova. 2020. A knowledge graph for industry 4.0. In *European Semantic Web Conference*, pages 465–480. Springer.

Georg Buchgeher, David Gabauer, Jorge Martinez-Gil, and Lisa Ehrlinger. 2021. Knowledge graphs in manufacturing and production: A systematic literature review. *IEEE Access*, 9:55537–55554.

Tzu-Yu Chen, Yu-Ching Chiu, Nanyi Bi, and Richard Tzong-Han Tsai. 2021. Multi-modal chatbot in intelligent manufacturing. *IEEE Access*, 9:82118–82129.

Bernardo Consoli and Renata Vieira. 2019. Multidomain contextual embeddings for named entity recognition. In *Proceedings of the Iberian Languages Evaluation Forum*, volume 2421, pages 434–441.

Joshua C Denny, Anderson Spickard III, Peter J Speltz, Renee Porier, Donna E Rosenstiel, and James S Powers. 2015. Using natural language processing to provide personalized learning opportunities from trainee clinical notes. *Journal of biomedical informatics*, 56:292–299.

Jacob Devlin, Ming-Wei Chang, Kenton Lee, and Kristina Toutanova. 2018. Bert: Pre-training of deep bidirectional transformers for language understanding. *arXiv preprint arXiv:1810.04805*.

Hassan Abdel-Gawad El-Hofy. 2005. *Advanced machining processes: nontraditional and hybrid machining processes*. McGraw Hill Professional.

Waguih ElMaraghy, Hoda ElMaraghy, Tetsuo Tomiyama, and Laszlo Monostori. 2012. Complexity in engineering design and manufacturing. *CIRP annals*, 61(2):793–814.

William E Frazier. 2014. Metal additive manufacturing: a review. *Journal of Materials Engineering and performance*, 23(6):1917–1928.

Martina Garofalo, Maria Angela Pellegrino, Abdulrahman Altabba, and Michael Cochez. 2018. Leveraging knowledge graph embedding techniques for industry 4.0 use cases. In *Cyber Defence in Industry 4.0 Systems and Related Logistics and IT Infrastructures*, pages 10–26. IOS Press.

Ian Gibson, David W Rosen, Brent Stucker, Mahyar Khorasani, David Rosen, Brent Stucker, and Mahyar Khorasani. 2021. *Additive manufacturing technologies*, volume 17. Springer.

Mikell P Groover. 2020. *Fundamentals of modern manufacturing: materials, processes, and systems*. John Wiley & Sons.

Daniel Hernández, Aidan Hogan, and Markus Krötzsch. 2015. Reifying rdf: What works well with wikidata? *SSWS@ ISWC*, 1457:32–47.

Hicham Hossayni, Imran Khan, Mohammad Aazam, Amin Taleghani-Isfahani, and Noel Crespi. 2020. Semkore: Improving machine maintenance in industrial iot with semantic knowledge graphs. *Applied Sciences*, 10(18):6325.

Manmeet Kaur and K Singh. 2019. Review on titanium and titanium based alloys as biomaterials for orthopaedic applications. *Materials Science and Engineering: C*, 102:844–862.

Sindo Kou. 2003. Welding metallurgy. *New Jersey, USA*, 431(446):223–225.

Markus Kraft and Andreas Eibeck. 2020. J-park simulator: Knowledge graph for industry 4.0. *Chemie Ingenieur Technik*, 92(7):967–977.

Aman Kumar and Swathi Dinakaran. 2021. Textbook to triples: Creating knowledge graph in the form of triples from ai textbook. *arXiv preprint arXiv:2111.10692*.

Aman Kumar and Binil Starly. 2021. "fabner": information extraction from manufacturing process science domain literature using named entity recognition. *Journal of Intelligent Manufacturing*, pages 1–15.

Xinyu Li, Chun-Hsien Chen, Pai Zheng, Zuoxu Wang, Zuhua Jiang, and Zhixing Jiang. 2020. A knowledge graph-aided concept–knowledge approach for evolutionary smart product–service system development. *Journal of Mechanical Design*, 142(10):101403.

Yunqing Li, Shivakumar Raman, Paul Cohen, and Binil Starly. 2021. Design of knowledge graph in manufacturing services discovery. In *International Manufacturing Science and Engineering Conference*, volume 85079, page V002T07A010. American Society of Mechanical Engineers.

Kun Liang, Baoxian Zhou, Yiying Zhang, Yiping Li, Bo Zhang, and Xiankun Zhang. 2022. Pf2rm: A power fault retrieval and recommendation model based on knowledge graph. *Energies*, 15(5):1810.

Shimin Liu, Yuqian Lu, Jie Li, Dengqiang Song, Xuemin Sun, and Jinsong Bao. 2021. Multi-scale evolution mechanism and knowledge construction of a digital twin mimic model. *Robotics and Computer-Integrated Manufacturing*, 71:102123.

Pablo N Mendes, Max Jakob, Andrés García-Silva, and Christian Bizer. 2011. Dbpedia spotlight: shedding light on the web of documents. In *Proceedings of the 7th international conference on semantic systems*, pages 1–8.

Aaron Meurer, Christopher P Smith, Mateusz Paprocki, Ondřej Čertík, Sergey B Kirpichev, Matthew Rocklin, AMiT Kumar, Sergiu Ivanov, Jason K Moore, Sartaj Singh, et al. 2017. Sympy: symbolic computing in python. *PeerJ Computer Science*, 3:e103.

Ercan Oztemel and Samet Gursev. 2020. Literature review of industry 4.0 and related technologies. *Journal of Intelligent Manufacturing*, 31(1):127–182.

Jeffrey Pennington, Richard Socher, and Christopher D Manning. 2014. Glove: Global vectors for word representation. In *Proceedings of the 2014 conference on empirical methods in natural language processing (EMNLP)*, pages 1532–1543.

Behnam Rahdari, Peter Brusilovsky, Khushboo Thaker, and Jordan Barria-Pineda. 2020. Using knowledge graph for explainable recommendation of external content in electronic textbooks. In *iTextbooks@ AIED*.

KP Rajurkar, H Hadidi, J Pariti, and GC Reddy. 2017. Review of sustainability issues in non-traditional machining processes. *Procedia Manufacturing*, 7:714–720.

Daniel Ringler and Heiko Paulheim. 2017. One knowledge graph to rule them all? analyzing the differences between dbpedia, yago, wikidata & co. In *Joint German/Austrian Conference on Artificial Intelligence (Künstliche Intelligenz)*, pages 366–372. Springer.

Martien A Cohen Stuart, Wilhelm TS Huck, Jan Genzer, Marcus Müller, Christopher Ober, Manfred Stamm, Gleb B Sukhorukov, Igal Szleifer, Vladimir V Tsukruk, Marek Urban, et al. 2010. Emerging applications of stimuli-responsive polymer materials. *Nature materials*, 9(2):101–113.

Tao Sun and Qi Wang. 2019. Multi-source fault detection and diagnosis based on multi-level knowledge graph and bayesian theory reasoning (s). In *SEKE*, pages 177–232.

Baicun Wang, S Jack Hu, Lei Sun, and Theodor Freiheit. 2020a. Intelligent welding system technologies: State-of-the-art review and perspectives. *Journal of Manufacturing Systems*, 56:373–391.

Qingyun Wang, Manling Li, Xuan Wang, Nikolaus Parulian, Guangxing Han, Jiawei Ma, Jingxuan Tu, Ying Lin, Haoran Zhang, Weili Liu, et al. 2020b. Covid-19 literature knowledge graph construction and drug repurposing report generation. *arXiv preprint arXiv:2007.00576*.

XiuQing Wang and ShunKun Yang. 2019. A tutorial and survey on fault knowledge graph. *Cyberspace Data and Intelligence, and Cyber-Living, Syndrome, and Health*, pages 256–271.

Kaufui V Wong and Aldo Hernandez. 2012. A review of additive manufacturing. *International scholarly research notices*, 2012.

Hehua Yan, Jun Yang, and Jiafu Wan. 2020. Knowime: a system to construct a knowledge graph for intelligent manufacturing equipment. *Ieee Access*, 8:41805–41813.

Qian Yan, Hanhua Dong, Jin Su, Jianhua Han, Bo Song, Qingsong Wei, and Yusheng Shi. 2018. A review of 3d printing technology for medical applications. *Engineering*, 4(5):729–742.

Yan Yang, Tianliang Hu, Yingxin Ye, Wenbin Gao, and Chengrui Zhang. 2019. A knowledge generation mechanism of machining process planning using cloud technology. *Journal of Ambient Intelligence and Humanized Computing*, 10(3):1081–1092.

Yingxin Ye, Tianliang Hu, Chengrui Zhang, and Weichao Luo. 2018. Design and development of a cnc machining process knowledge base using cloud technology. *The International Journal of Advanced Manufacturing Technology*, 94(9):3413–3425.

Tianyu Zhao, Yan Huang, Songfan Yang, Yuyu Luo, Jianhua Feng, Yong Wang, Haitao Yuan, Kang Pan, Kaiyu Li, Haoda Li, et al. 2019. Mathgraph: A knowledge graph for automatically solving mathematical exercises. In *International conference on database systems for advanced applications*, pages 760–776. Springer.

Bin Zhou, Jinsong Bao, Jie Li, Yuqian Lu, Tianyuan Liu, and Qiwan Zhang. 2021. A novel knowledge graph-based optimization approach for resource allocation in discrete manufacturing workshops. *Robotics and Computer-Integrated Manufacturing*, 71:102160.

Zude Zhou, Shane Xie, and Dejun Chen. 2012. *Fundamentals of digital manufacturing science*. Springer.

Zicheng Zhu, Vimal G Dhokia, Aydin Nassehi, and Stephen T Newman. 2013. A review of hybrid manufacturing processes–state of the art and future perspectives. *International Journal of Computer Integrated Manufacturing*, 26(7):596–615.

Modeling Compositionality with Dependency Graph for Dialogue Generation

Xiaofeng Chen[1], **Yirong Chen**[1], **Xiaofen Xing**[1]*, **Xiangmin Xu**[1], **Wenjing Han**[1], **Qianfeng Tie**[1]
[1]UBTECH-SCUT Joint Research Lab, School of Electronic and Information Engineering,
South China University of Technology, China
{eexiaofengchen, eeyirongchen, eewenjinghh, 202120112795}@mail.scut.edu.cn
{xmxu, xfxing}@scut.edu.cn

Abstract

Because of the compositionality of natural language, syntactic structure which contains the information about the relationship between words is a key factor for semantic understanding. However, the widely adopted Transformer is hard to learn the syntactic structure effectively in dialogue generation tasks. To explicitly model the compositionaity of language in Transformer Block, we restrict the information flow between words by constructing directed dependency graph and propose Dependency Relation Attention (DRA). Experimental results demonstrate that DRA can further improve the performance of state-of-the-art models for dialogue generation.

1 Introduction

In natural language, complex semantics are often expressed by combining words with certain rules. For example, "room" can express higher-level semantics by fusing the information of "a" and "hotel", and the meaning of "reserve" will be clearer after fusing the information of "room". Prior works have achieved great success in NLP tasks by leveraging syntactic structure knowledge, such as semantic relatedness (Tai et al., 2015; Gupta and Zhang, 2018), sentiment analysis (Ma et al., 2015; Sun et al., 2019), relation extraction (Tian et al., 2021), and named entity recognition (Aguilar and Solorio, 2019; Xu et al., 2021).

Due to the strong ability to capture long-term dependencies (Tang et al., 2018), many recent works have adopted the Transformer block (Vaswani et al., 2017) to extract context features in dialogue generation tasks (Su et al., 2019; Liu et al., 2020; Song et al., 2021). However, it is hard for Transformer block to implicitly learn the compositionality of language in the training process of dialog generation, since it simply uses position embeddings to represent the relationships between words, and it learns

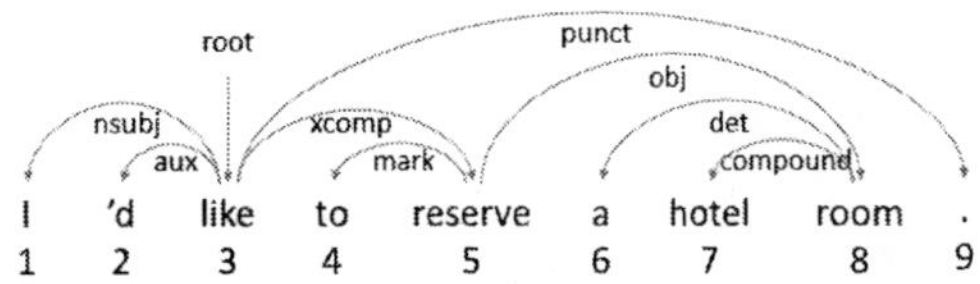

Figure 1: An example of dependency graph.

the local position information that can only be effective in masked language modeling (Wang and Chen, 2020). Besides, the computation of attention weights on unrelated word pairs in Transformer block is redundant and decreases performance.

To obtain better distributed representations of context in dialogue generation tasks, we propose Dependency Relation Attention to model the relationship between words as an alternative to position embeddings. Specifically, we incorporate dependency relation knowledge that contains syntactic structure information into the Transformer block. As shown in Figure 1, we use the dependency parser (Chen and Manning, 2014) in the StanfordCoreNLP toolkit (Manning et al., 2014) to build dependency graphs of utterances. Then, the Dependency Relation Mask is generated to avoid performing attention on words without dependency relations, and the fusion of information among words depends on the direction specified by the dependency graph. Our contributions can be summarized as follows:

- We propose Dependency Relation Attention, a novel method for expressing relationships between words as an alternative to position embeddings.
- We demonstrate that our method can further improve the performance of Transformer and DialogBERT (Gu et al., 2021) in dialogue generation task by conducting experiments on two datasets.

* Corresponding author: xfxing@scut.edu.cn

Proceedings of the Workshop on Structured and Unstructured Knowledge Integration (SUKI), pages 9 - 16
July 14, 2022 ©2022 Association for Computational Linguistics

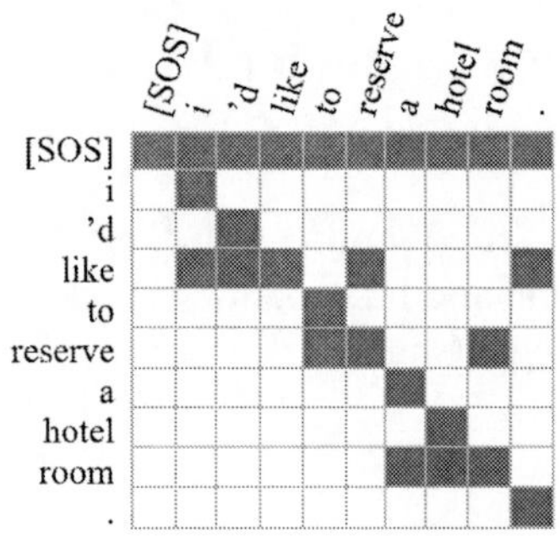

Figure 2: Dependency Relation Mask.

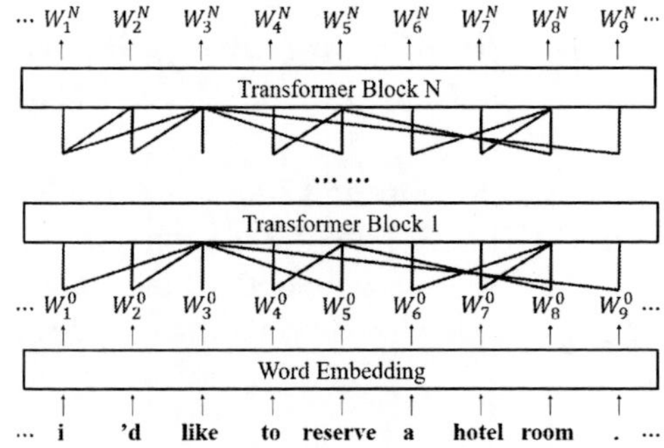

Figure 3: Illustration of applying DRA to standard Transformer encoder. Dependency Relation Mask is used to model the semantic relationship between words instead of position embeddings.

2 Related Works

In the past few years, dependency graph has drawn attention from many researchers in the field of NLP. Strubell et al. (2018) propose Syntactically-informed self-attention and incorporate syntactic dependency knowledge into a attention head of specific Transformer block. To make the attention learned by Transformer more interpretable, Wang et al. (2019) propose Constituent Attention which makes each position not attend to the position in different constituents. Ahmad et al. (2021) explicitly fuse structural information to learn the dependency relations between words with different syntactic distances.

In dialogue generation tasks, to improve the quality of generated responses, previous works focus on capturing the high-level relationships between contexts and responses (Xing et al., 2018; Zhang et al., 2019) or between utterances in context(Gu et al., 2021). How to effectively model the relationships between words in Transformer has not been explored. Inspired by TreeLSTM (Tai et al., 2015), our method aim at modeling the compositionality in language, then the Transformer block does not need to learn the relationships between words through position embeddings in the training process of dialog generation. The differences between DRA and others dependency relation-aware attention mechanisms are: (1) DRA incorporates the dependency arc directions into Transformer block to model the relationships between words instead of position embeddings. (2) The position embeddings are excluded for the models with DRA applied.

3 Method

In dialogue generation tasks, given a piece of context containing m utterances $U = \{X_1, ..., X_m\}$ as inputs, where $X_i = \{x_{i,1}, ..., x_{i,n_i}\}, i \in [1, m]$ indicates the i-th utterance containing n_i words, dialogue generation models map it into feature vectors and estimate the generation probability of the corresponding response $Y = \{y_1, ..., y_t\}$:

$$p(y_1, ..., y_t|U) = \prod_{k=1}^{t} p(y_k|y_{<k}, U) \quad (1)$$

To obtain a better representations of context, we incorporate dependency relation knowledge into the Transformer block, which is widely used in recent works.

3.1 Dependency Relation Mask

We use the StanfordCoreNLP toolkit[1] to parse the dependency relations and obtain a set of triples $R_{i,j} = (r_{i,j}, g_{i,j}, d_{i,j}), j \in [1, n_i]$ for each utterance, where $r_{i,j}$, $g_{i,j}$, and $d_{i,j}$ represent the name of the relation, the index of the governor, and the index of the dependent (the j-th word in the i-th utterance) respectively. For the utterance in Figure 1, here is the triples R returned from the parser:

•$(nsubj, 3, 1)$ •$(aux, 3, 2)$ •$(ROOT, 0, 3)$
•$(mark, 5, 4)$ •$(xcomp, 3, 5)$ •$(det, 8, 6)$
•$(compound, 8, 7)$ •$(obj, 5, 8)$ •$(punct, 3, 9)$

The indexes in dependency relation triples $E = \{(g_1, d_1), ..., (g_n, d_n)\}$ are used to generate the Dependency Relation Mask $M \in \mathbb{R}^{(n+1)\times(n+1)}$. Figure 2 shows an example:

$$M_{u,v} = \begin{cases} 0, & u = 0 \quad or \quad u = v \\ 0, & (u, v) \in E \\ -\infty, & otherwise \end{cases} \quad (2)$$

3.2 Dependency Relation Attention

The main idea of our proposed method is to use Dependency Relation Attention (DRA) to model

[1] https://nlp.stanford.edu/software/nndep.html

the compositionality, instead of letting models implicitly learn the relationships between words through position embeddings. Figure 3 is an illustration of applying Dependency Relation Attention to a standard Transformer encoder. Specifically, for the l-th layer of the Transformer block in the encoding process, the hidden states of words $W^l \in \mathbb{R}^{n \times d_{hidden}}$ are linearly mapped to three subspaces in different heads of multi-head attention network: $Q^l \in \mathbb{R}^{n \times d_{head}}$, $K^l \in \mathbb{R}^{n \times d_{head}}$ and $V^l \in \mathbb{R}^{n \times d_{head}}$. The attention score matrix $S^l \in \mathbb{R}^{n \times n}$, which indicates the strength of relationships between words, is calculated by:

$$S^l = \frac{Q^l K^{lT}}{\sqrt{d_{head}}} \tag{3}$$

Then, the attention scores of unrelated word pairs are masked:

$$S^l_{masked} = S^l + M \tag{4}$$

The hidden states of words W are updated based on the dependency relations:

$$\begin{aligned} A^l_{masked} &= softmax(S^l_{masked}) \\ O^{l,i} &= A^{l,i}_{masked} V^{l,i} \\ O^l &= concat(O^{l,1}, ..., O^{l,n_{head}}) \\ W^{l+1} &= W^l + O^l \end{aligned} \tag{5}$$

4 Experiments

4.1 Settings

4.1.1 Datasets

In our experiment, we use DailyDialog (Li et al., 2017) and EmpatheticDialogues (Rashkin et al., 2019) to verify the effectiveness of our method. They contains 11.1K, 1K, 1K and 19.5K, 2.7K, 2.5K dialogues for training, validation, testing, respectively. To accommodate the granularity of the word segmentation of the dependency parser and ensure fairness, StanfordCoreNLP toolkit is used to tokenize utterances for all models. Besides, we report the results of methods with subword tokenization in appendix. Words with word frequency less than 3 are replaced by "[UNK]". For each sample, dialogue turn and utterance length are limited to 4 and 50, respectively.

4.1.2 Compared Methods

We apply DRA to Transformer (Vaswani et al., 2017) and DialogBERT (Gu et al., 2021) and position embeddings are excluded. The performance of models before and after the modification and the following methods are compared: ReCoSa (Zhang et al., 2019), LISA (Strubell et al., 2018), Tree-Transformer (Wang et al., 2019) and GATE (Ahmad et al., 2021). Position embeddings are included for all baseline models.

We set the hidden sizes of all models to 768. The number of Transformer layers is set to 3. Each Transformer block contains 16 attention heads. The word embedding layers of all models are initialized with GloVe 300-dimensional word embeddings (Pennington et al., 2014). The batch size is set to 40. All models are trained by the AdamW (Loshchilov and Hutter, 2018) optimizer with weight decay of 0.01. We linearly warm up the learning rate from 0 to 5e-4 at the first 3000 steps. Afterward, the learning rate decreases to 0 linearly during training.

4.1.3 Evaluation Metrics

Automatic evaluation. PPL, BLEU (Papineni et al., 2002) and Distinct (Li et al., 2016) are employed to reflect the degree of fluency, relevance and diversity of generated responses respectively. They are widely used in dialog generation tasks (Song et al., 2020; Liang et al., 2021).

Human evaluation. We randomly select 100 contexts from the DailyDialog test set and generate responses with models trained on DailyDialog. Based on grammatical correctness and contextual coherence, three annotators are asked to score the generated responses independently with the following grading scale: "+0" (response is not fluent), "+1" (response is fluent but irrelevant), and "+2" (response is fluent and relevant).

4.2 Experimental Results

Table 1 gives the automatic evaluation results on DailyDialog and EmpatheticDialogues validation set. For both datasets, Transformer+DRA and DialogBERT+DRA achieved the best performance on PPL and Dist-2 respectively. Transformer+DRA achieved comparable BLEU-2 scores in contrast to DialogBERT+DRA. It is worth noting that DRA improved the performance of Transformer and DialogBERT on all automatic metrics, which indicates that our method can help these two models generate more fluent, relevant, and diverse responses. We also study the computational efficiency and the impact of parsing errors, the results are shown in appendix.

The results of human evaluation are shown in

Model	DailyDialog			EmpatheticDialogues		
	PPL	BLEU-2	Dist-2	PPL	BLEU-2	Dist-2
ReCoSa	19.846	20.538	16.611	34.450	19.062	7.619
LISA	18.378	19.002	17.011	32.467	19.169	6.974
TreeTransformer	18.155	20.035	17.847	31.862	19.755	7.870
GATE ($\delta = 1$)	18.405	19.142	17.742	32.273	18.640	7.452
Transformer	18.278	19.519	17.381	32.329	18.553	7.499
Transformer+DRA	**17.628**	21.140	18.396	**31.604**	**19.966**	8.203
DialogBERT	20.056	18.069	15.562	35.643	17.199	5.064
DialogBERT+DRA	17.878	**21.786**	**21.283**	32.785	19.739	**9.601**

Table 1: Automatic evaluation results on DailyDialog and EmpatheticDialogues validation set.

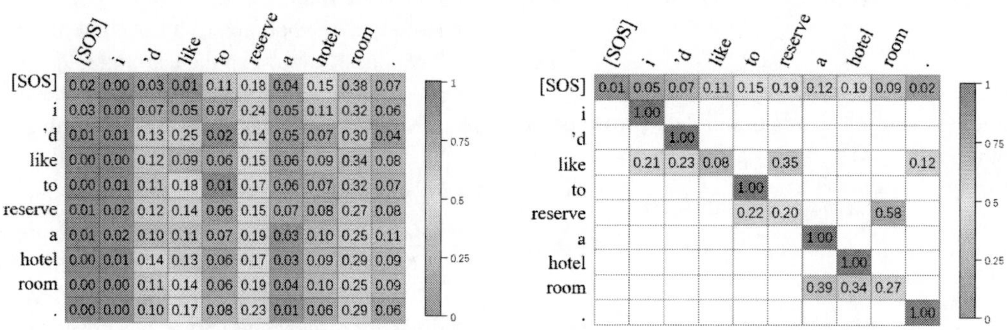

(a) Standard Transformer.

(b) Transformer+DRA.

Figure 4: The average attention weights of the last layer of Transformer encoder in different methods.

Model	+2	+1	+0	Avg.
ReCoSa	29.7	52.7	17.7	1.12
LISA	35.3	51.7	13.0	1.22
TreeTransformer	32.3	55.3	12.3	1.20
GATE ($\delta = 1$)	32.7	55.0	12.3	1.20
Transformer	33.3	54.3	12.3	1.21
Transformer+DRA	47.0	39.0	14.0	1.33
DialogBERT	32.3	59.3	8.3	1.24
DialogBERT+DRA	50.0	43.3	6.7	**1.43**

Table 2: Human evaluation results. (in %)

Table 2. The Fleiss' kappa score (Fleiss, 1971) for assessing agreement among annotators was 0.563, which can be interpreted as "moderate agreement". This shows that DRA can enhance the semantic understanding of Transformer block and help models generate more relevant responses, especially for the hierarchical Transformer encoder architecture.

4.3 Discussions

To further explore why our method can improve the performance of the Transformer encoder, we visualized the attention weights of the last layer of the Transformer encoder in different methods. Taking the utterance in Figure 1 as input, Figure 4 shows the mean value of attention weights of 16 heads in standard Transformer and Transformer+DRA. We can see that, in standard Transformer, the Transformer block assigns very similar weights to each part of the utterance when updating the hidden state of different words. This means that standard Transformer encoder can find the key parts of the utterance, but does not learn the relationships between words. In Transformer+DRA, for each word, attention weights are assigned to appropriate parts. For example, when updating the hidden state of "reserve", the Transformer block pays more attention to the "room" that has merged the information of "a" and "hotel". In other words, DRA makes it easier for Transformer encoder to understand the relationships between words and generate more meaningful distributed representations.

5 Conclusion and Future Work

In this paper, we propose Dependency Relation Attention (DRA) to model the relationships between words instead of position embeddings in the Transformer encoder. Experimental results show that our method can further improve the performance of models that use Transformer block to obtain the distributed representations of context in dialogue generation task. In the future, we will study the effect of the specific domains that parsers are usually trained in, as well as the possibility of improving the performance of pretrained language models with DRA.

6 Acknowledgement

The work is supported in part by the National Natural Science Foundation of China under Grant U1801262; in part by the Key-Area Research and Development Program of Guangdong under Grant 2019B010154003; in part by the Science and Technology Project of Guangzhou under Grant 202103010002; and in part by the Guangdong Provincial Key Laboratory of Human Digital Twin under Grant 2022B1212010004.

References

Gustavo Aguilar and Thamar Solorio. 2019. Dependency-aware named entity recognition with relative and global attentions. *arXiv e-prints*, pages arXiv–1909.

Wasi Uddin Ahmad, Nanyun Peng, and Kai-Wei Chang. 2021. Gate: graph attention transformer encoder for cross-lingual relation and event extraction. In *Proceedings of the Thirty-Fifth AAAI Conference on Artificial Intelligence*, volume 4, pages 74–75.

Danqi Chen and Christopher D Manning. 2014. A fast and accurate dependency parser using neural networks. In *Proceedings of the 2014 conference on empirical methods in natural language processing (EMNLP)*, pages 740–750.

Joseph L Fleiss. 1971. Measuring nominal scale agreement among many raters. *Psychological bulletin*, 76(5):378.

Xiaodong Gu, Kang Min Yoo, and Jung-Woo Ha. 2021. Dialogbert: Discourse-aware response generation via learning to recover and rank utterances. In *Proceedings of the AAAI Conference on Artificial Intelligence*, volume 35, pages 12911–12919.

Amulya Gupta and Zhu Zhang. 2018. To attend or not to attend: A case study on syntactic structures for semantic relatedness. In *Proceedings of the 56th Annual Meeting of the Association for Computational Linguistics (Volume 1: Long Papers)*, pages 2116–2125.

Jiwei Li, Will Monroe, Alan Ritter, Dan Jurafsky, Michel Galley, and Jianfeng Gao. 2016. Deep reinforcement learning for dialogue generation. In *Proceedings of the 2016 Conference on Empirical Methods in Natural Language Processing*, pages 1192–1202, Austin, Texas. Association for Computational Linguistics.

Yanran Li, Hui Su, Xiaoyu Shen, Wenjie Li, Ziqiang Cao, and Shuzi Niu. 2017. Dailydialog: A manually labelled multi-turn dialogue dataset. In *Proceedings of the Eighth International Joint Conference on Natural Language Processing (Volume 1: Long Papers)*, pages 986–995.

Yunlong Liang, Fandong Meng, Ying Zhang, Yufeng Chen, Jinan Xu, and Jie Zhou. 2021. Infusing multisource knowledge with heterogeneous graph neural network for emotional conversation generation. In *Proceedings of the AAAI Conference on Artificial Intelligence*, volume 35, pages 13343–13352.

Qian Liu, Yihong Chen, Bei Chen, Jian-Guang Lou, Zixuan Chen, Bin Zhou, and Dongmei Zhang. 2020. You impress me: Dialogue generation via mutual persona perception. In *Proceedings of the 58th Annual Meeting of the Association for Computational Linguistics*, pages 1417–1427.

Ilya Loshchilov and Frank Hutter. 2018. Fixing weight decay regularization in adam.

Mingbo Ma, Liang Huang, Bowen Zhou, and Bing Xiang. 2015. Dependency-based convolutional neural networks for sentence embedding. In *Proceedings of the 53rd Annual Meeting of the Association for Computational Linguistics and the 7th International Joint Conference on Natural Language Processing (Volume 2: Short Papers)*, pages 174–179.

Christopher D Manning, Mihai Surdeanu, John Bauer, Jenny Rose Finkel, Steven Bethard, and David McClosky. 2014. The stanford corenlp natural language processing toolkit. In *Proceedings of 52nd annual meeting of the association for computational linguistics: system demonstrations*, pages 55–60.

Kishore Papineni, Salim Roukos, Todd Ward, and Wei-Jing Zhu. 2002. Bleu: a method for automatic evaluation of machine translation. In *Proceedings of the 40th Annual Meeting of the Association for Computational Linguistics*, pages 311–318, Philadelphia, Pennsylvania, USA. Association for Computational Linguistics.

Jeffrey Pennington, Richard Socher, and Christopher Manning. 2014. GloVe: Global vectors for word representation. In *Proceedings of the 2014 Conference on Empirical Methods in Natural Language Processing (EMNLP)*, pages 1532–1543, Doha, Qatar. Association for Computational Linguistics.

Hannah Rashkin, Eric Michael Smith, Margaret Li, and Y-Lan Boureau. 2019. Towards empathetic open-domain conversation models: A new benchmark and dataset. In *Proceedings of the 57th Annual Meeting of the Association for Computational Linguistics*, pages 5370–5381.

Haoyu Song, Yan Wang, Kaiyan Zhang, Wei-Nan Zhang, and Ting Liu. 2021. BoB: BERT over BERT for training persona-based dialogue models from limited personalized data. In *Proceedings of the 59th Annual Meeting of the Association for Computational Linguistics and the 11th International Joint Conference on Natural Language Processing (Volume 1: Long Papers)*, pages 167–177, Online. Association for Computational Linguistics.

Haoyu Song, Yan Wang, Weinan Zhang, Xiaojiang Liu, and Ting Liu. 2020. Generate, delete and rewrite: A three-stage framework for improving persona consistency of dialogue generation. In *Proceedings of the 58th Annual Meeting of the Association for Computational Linguistics*, pages 5821–5831.

Emma Strubell, Patrick Verga, Daniel Andor, David Weiss, and Andrew McCallum. 2018. Linguistically-informed self-attention for semantic role labeling. In *Proceedings of the 2018 Conference on Empirical Methods in Natural Language Processing*, pages 5027–5038.

Hui Su, Xiaoyu Shen, Rongzhi Zhang, Fei Sun, Pengwei Hu, Cheng Niu, and Jie Zhou. 2019. Improving multi-turn dialogue modelling with utterance rewriter. In *Proceedings of the 57th Annual Meeting of the Association for Computational Linguistics*, pages 22–31.

Kai Sun, Richong Zhang, Samuel Mensah, Yongyi Mao, and Xudong Liu. 2019. Aspect-level sentiment analysis via convolution over dependency tree. In *Proceedings of the 2019 Conference on Empirical Methods in Natural Language Processing and the 9th International Joint Conference on Natural Language Processing (EMNLP-IJCNLP)*, pages 5679–5688, Hong Kong, China. Association for Computational Linguistics.

Kai Sheng Tai, Richard Socher, and Christopher D Manning. 2015. Improved semantic representations from tree-structured long short-term memory networks. In *Proceedings of the 53rd Annual Meeting of the Association for Computational Linguistics and the 7th International Joint Conference on Natural Language Processing (Volume 1: Long Papers)*, pages 1556–1566.

Gongbo Tang, Mathias Müller, Annette Rios Gonzales, and Rico Sennrich. 2018. Why self-attention? a targeted evaluation of neural machine translation architectures. In *Proceedings of the 2018 Conference on Empirical Methods in Natural Language Processing*, pages 4263–4272.

Yuanhe Tian, Guimin Chen, Yan Song, and Xiang Wan. 2021. Dependency-driven relation extraction with attentive graph convolutional networks. In *Proceedings of the 59th Annual Meeting of the Association for Computational Linguistics and the 11th International Joint Conference on Natural Language Processing (Volume 1: Long Papers)*, pages 4458–4471, Online. Association for Computational Linguistics.

Ashish Vaswani, Noam Shazeer, Niki Parmar, Jakob Uszkoreit, Llion Jones, Aidan N Gomez, Łukasz Kaiser, and Illia Polosukhin. 2017. Attention is all you need. In *Advances in neural information processing systems*, pages 5998–6008.

Yaushian Wang, Hung-Yi Lee, and Yun-Nung Chen. 2019. Tree transformer: Integrating tree structures into self-attention. In *Proceedings of the 2019 Conference on Empirical Methods in Natural Language Processing and the 9th International Joint Conference on Natural Language Processing (EMNLP-IJCNLP)*, pages 1061–1070.

Yu-An Wang and Yun-Nung Chen. 2020. What do position embeddings learn? an empirical study of pre-trained language model positional encoding. In *Proceedings of the 2020 Conference on Empirical Methods in Natural Language Processing (EMNLP)*, pages 6840–6849.

Chen Xing, Yu Wu, Wei Wu, Yalou Huang, and Ming Zhou. 2018. Hierarchical recurrent attention network for response generation. In *Proceedings of the AAAI Conference on Artificial Intelligence*, volume 32.

Lu Xu, Zhanming Jie, Wei Lu, and Lidong Bing. 2021. Better feature integration for named entity recognition. In *Proceedings of the 2021 Conference of the North American Chapter of the Association for Computational Linguistics: Human Language Technologies*, pages 3457–3469.

Hainan Zhang, Yanyan Lan, Liang Pang, Jiafeng Guo, and Xueqi Cheng. 2019. ReCoSa: Detecting the relevant contexts with self-attention for multi-turn dialogue generation. In *Proceedings of the 57th Annual Meeting of the Association for Computational Linguistics*, pages 3721–3730, Florence, Italy. Association for Computational Linguistics.

A Additional Analysis

Extra experiments were conducted to further analyse models that applied with DRA, position embedding (*PE.*), or subword-level tokenization (*ST.*), since DRA and PE. can be applied to transformer block at the same time. The result is shown in Table 3 (*Trans.*, *Dial.*, *B-2* and *D-2* denote Transformer, DialogBERT, BLEU-2 and Dist-2, respectively). *ST.* can not improve the fluency (PPL) and diversity (D-2) of generated responses although it can promote higher BLEU score. Besides, the models with DRA can not handle the information of position embeddings well, we need to design some methods that can model the information of word order in dependency graph in the future.

Model	DailyDialog		
	PPL	B-2	D-2
Transformer	18.28	19.52	17.38
- Trans.+ST.	18.59	**22.15**	16.64
- Trans.+DRA	**17.63**	21.14	**18.40**
- Trans.+DRA+PE.	18.13	19.66	18.08
DialogBERT	20.06	18.07	15.56
- Dial.+ST.	20.07	19.51	15.72
- Dial.+DRA	**17.88**	**21.79**	**21.28**
- Dial.+DRA+PE.	20.32	17.86	15.77

Table 3: Result of extra comparison.

B Comparison of Running Time

Table 4 shows the average time occupied by different models to generating response for each dialogue in DailyDialog (*Pre.* denote the process of word tokenization and dependency relation parsing of the raw text, *Gen.* denote the process of inference). We can see that the dependency parsing process does not take much time.

Model	Pre.	Gen.	Total
Transformer	0.005s	0.111s	0.116s
Transformer+DRA	0.028s	0.115s	0.143s
DialogBERT	0.005s	0.123s	0.128s
DialogBERT+DRA	0.030s	0.118s	0.148s

Table 4: Comparison of running time.

C Results of Parsing Errors.

As the accuracy of dependency parsing will affect the downstream task performance, it is worthwhile to investigate the result of the errors that result from syntactic parsing. We simulate parsing errors by manually changing the parsing results, specifically, the attention weights with dependency relations will be masked and those without dependency relations will not. Figure 5 show how the parsing errors affect PPL, BLEU-2, Dist-2 of models on DailyDialog validation set. The horizontal axis in the figure represents the proportion of parsing errors. It shows that our proposed method has certain robustness, especially for the hierarchical Transformer encoder architecture.

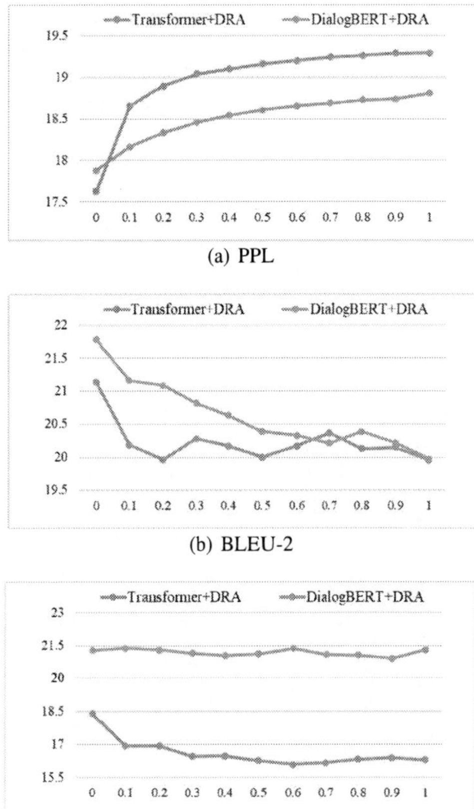

(a) PPL

(b) BLEU-2

(c) Dist-2

Figure 5: The result of parsing errors.

D Samples of Generated Dialogues

Table 5 and 6 provide some examples of the generated responses. The visual attention weights of different methods are presented in Figure 6 and 7. The models with DRA will focus on the relevant words when updating the hidden state of each word. They demonstrates that Dependency Relation Attention can help Transformer and DialogBERT generate better responses.

Example 1	
Speaker1:	Hello, Miao Li, where are you going?
Speaker2:	Hello, I am going to the store to buy some fruit.
Gold Resp:	Oh, would you do me a favor?
Transformer:	Oh, I'm afraid I'm going to take the train station.
Transformer+DRA:	What kind of fruit do you like?
DialogBERT:	Would you like some dessert?
DialogBERT+DRA:	What are you going to buy?

Table 5: Example responses from different models.

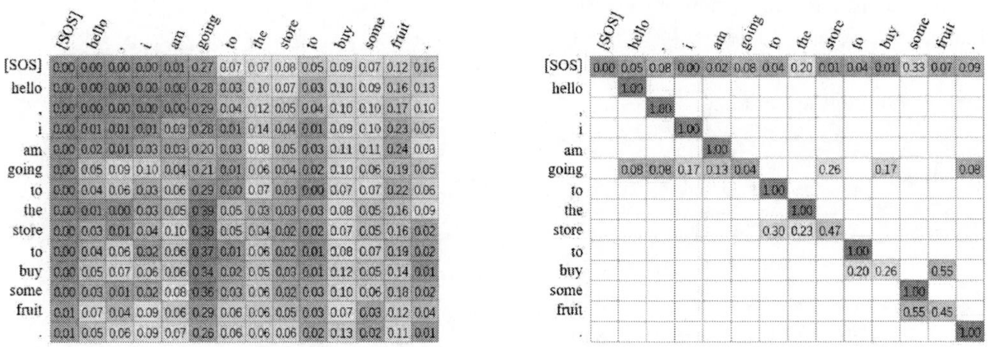

(a) Standard Transformer. (b) Transformer+DRA.

Figure 6: Attention weights visualization of example 1

Example 2	
Speaker1:	My niece is super talented lately.
Speaker2:	What is her best talent?
Speaker1:	Art, she was accepted into a special program for high school.
Gold Resp:	Does she draw or paint? How many students are in this program?
Transformer:	Wow, that is a pretty cool name.
Transformer+DRA:	Oh wow, that is impressive.
DialogBERT:	That's great. What kind of job?
DialogBERT+DRA:	Wow, that is a big accomplishment.

Table 6: Example responses from different models.

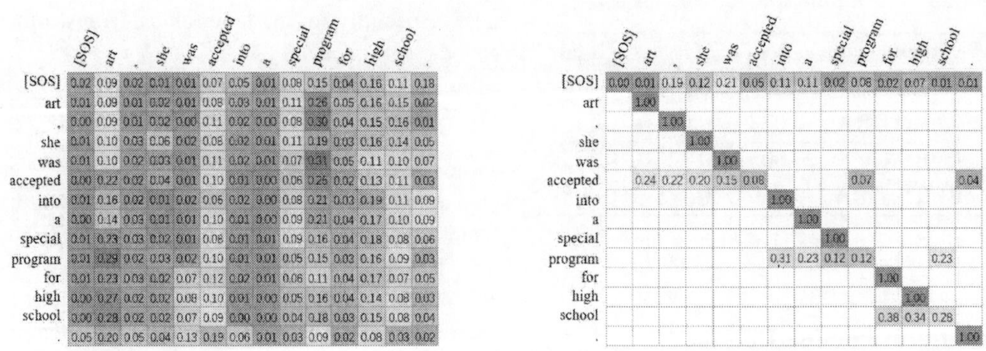

(a) Standard Transformer. (b) Transformer+DRA.

Figure 7: Attention weights visualization of example 2

Strategies to Improve Few-shot Learning for Intent Classification and Slot-Filling

Samyadeep Basu*, Karine lp Kiun Chong*, Amr Sharaf*, Alex Fischer, Vishal Rohra, Michael Amoake, Hazem El-Hammamy, Ehi Nosakhare, Vijay Ramani, Benjamin Han
{sbasu, kaipkiun, amrsharaf, alex.fischer, virohra, miamoako, haelhamm, ehnosakh, vijayram, diha}@microsoft.com
Microsoft AI

Abstract

Intent classification (IC) and slot filling (SF) are two fundamental tasks in modern Natural Language Understanding (NLU) systems. Collecting and annotating large amounts of data to train deep learning models for such systems are not scalable. This problem can be addressed by learning from few examples using fast supervised meta-learning techniques such as prototypical networks. In this work, we systematically investigate how contrastive learning and data augmentation methods can benefit these existing meta-learning pipelines for jointly modelled IC/SF tasks. Through extensive experiments across standard IC/SF benchmarks (SNIPS and ATIS), we show that our proposed approaches outperform standard meta-learning methods: contrastive losses as a regularizer in conjunction with prototypical networks consistently outperform the existing state-of-the-art for both IC and SF tasks, while data augmentation strategies primarily improve few-shot IC by a significant margin.

1 Introduction

NLU specific intent classification and slot-filling models often need to learn from only a few contextual examples given by the end user in industrial model deployment scenarios. Such models are often trained using meta-learning, a competitive few-shot learning strategy to learn from only a few examples. In this paper, we systematically dissect the existing meta-learning pipelines for jointly modelled few-shot Intent Classification (IC) and Slot Filling (SF) and identify practical training strategies to improve their performance by a significant margin. Precisely, we investigate how different data augmentation and contrastive learning strategies improve IC/SF performance, and show that our training approach outperforms state-of-the-art models for few-shot IC/SF. Given the user utterance: "*Book me a table for 6 at Lebanese Taverna*", an IC model identifies "*Restaurant Booking*" as the intent of interest, and an SF model identifies the slot types and values: *Party_Size:"6", Name: "Lebanese Taverna"*. These functionalities are typically driven by powerful deep learning models that rely on huge amounts of domain-specific training data. As such labeled data is rarely available, building models that can learn from only a few examples per class is inevitable.

Few-shot learning techniques (Krone et al., 2020; Ren and Xue, 2020; Geng et al., 2019, 2020; Liu et al., 2020b) have been recently proposed to address the problem of generalizing to unseen classes in IC/SF when only a few training examples per class are available. Krone et al. (2020) utilized meta-learning approaches such as prototypical networks (Snell et al., 2017) and MAML (Finn et al., 2017) to jointly model IC/SF. They showed that prototypical networks outperform other prevalent meta-learning techniques such as MAML as well as fine-tuning. Moreover, one primary benefit of prototypical networks is that it is computationally cheap during meta-testing, thus making it a good candidate for industrial few-shot learning systems. In this paper, we extend this powerful supervised meta-learning technique with unsupervised contrastive learning and data augmentation.

Rajendran et al. (2020) showed that meta-learners can be particular prone to overfitting which can be partially alleviated by data augmentation (Liu et al., 2020a). Data augmentation strategies in NLP have been shown to boost performance in general text classification settings (Wei and Zou, 2019b; Xie et al., 2019; Lee et al., 2021), however, there exists very little work on how data augmentation can be effectively used in the meta-learning pipeline specific to NLU tasks. To address this question, we first use a data augmentation strategy `slot-list values` for IC/SF tasks which generates synthetic utterances using dictionary-based slot-values. We note that similar dictionary based augmentation has been previously used in (Li et al.,

Proceedings of the Workshop on Structured and Unstructured Knowledge Integration (SUKI), pages 17 - 25
July 14, 2022

2021), but in the context of dialogue state tracking, orthogonal to our use-case. Additionally, we investigate how state-of-the-art augmentation strategies such as backtranslation (Xie et al., 2019) and perturbation-based augmentations such as EDA – Easy Data Augmentation (Wei and Zou, 2019b) – can be used alongside prototypical networks.

We further investigate how contrastive learning (Chen et al., 2020) can be used as a regularizer during the meta-training stage to create better generalizable meta-learners. Contrastive learning is useful in creating improved prototypes as they pull similar representations together while pushing apart dissimilar ones. Through extensive experiments across SNIPS and ATIS, we show that meta-training with contrastive losses as a regularizer improves IC/SF performance for unseen classes with few examples. Our contributions include:

- We demonstrate the effectiveness of contrastive losses as a regularizer in meta-learning, by empirically showing how it improves few-shot IC/SF tasks across benchmark datasets.
- We illustrate the positive impact of data augmentation techniques such as `slot-list values`, backtranslation and EDA in the meta-learning pipeline.

2 Proposed Approaches

We follow the few-shot learning setup for IC/SF described in (Krone et al., 2020) with a few modifications. Instead of using a frozen backbone such as BERT or ELMo with a BiLSTM head, we use a more powerful pre-trained RoBERTa encoder. Additionally, in contrast to (Krone et al., 2020), we update our encoder during the meta-training stage. For a given utterance $x^i = \{x^i_1, x^i_2, ..., x^i_n\}$ with n tokens, we first use the RoBERTa model denoted by f_ϕ to encode the utterance resulting in $h^i = \{h^i_{<cls>}, h^i_1, ..., h^i_n\}$. We use the `<cls>` token embedding to denote the utterance level embedding which we use for intent classification. For slot filling, we use each of the token embeddings $\{h^i_j\}^n_{j=1}$ of the ith utterance. Given a support set S, assuming S_l consists of utterances belonging to the intent class c_l and S_a consists of tokens from the slot class c_a, we first compute the class prototypes for intents (c_l) and slots (c_a):

$$c_l = \frac{1}{|S_l|} \sum_{x^i \in S_l} f_\phi(x^i) \tag{1}$$

$$c_a = \frac{1}{|S_a|} \sum_{x^i_j \in S_a} f_\phi(x^i_j) \quad \forall x^i \in S \tag{2}$$

Given a query example $\mathbf{z}$ and a distance function d, a distribution over the different classes is computed using the softmax of the distances to the different class prototypes. Specifically we denote the intent specific log likelihood loss as:

$$L_{IC}(\phi, \mathbf{z}) = -\log\{\frac{\exp(-d(f_\phi(\mathbf{z}), c_l))}{\sum_{l'} \exp(-d(f_\phi(\mathbf{z}), c_{l'}))}\} \tag{3}$$

We use euclidean distance as the standard distance function. Similarly, we define the slot specific loss as $L_{Slots}(\phi, \mathbf{z})$. For a given query set Q, the cumulative loss for intents and slots is the log likelihood averaged across all the query samples and is denoted by $L_{Total}(\phi)$:

$$L_{Total}(\phi) = \sum_{\mathbf{z} \in Q} \frac{1}{|Q|}\{L_{IC}(\phi, \mathbf{z}) + L_{Slots}(\phi, \mathbf{z})\} \tag{4}$$

2.1 Contrastive Learning

The general idea of contrastive learning (Chen et al., 2020) is to pull together the representations of similar samples while pushing apart the representations of dissimilar samples in an embedding space. In our work, we specifically incorporate the supervised contrastive loss as an added regularizer with the prototypical loss computation in Eq. (4). In particular we identify places in the meta-training pipeline where the incorporation of the contrastive loss is most beneficial for good generalization to few-shot classes. We devise two types of contrastive losses for the IC/SF tasks: (a) contrastive loss for intents $L_{contrastiveIC}(\phi)$ where the `<cls>` token embedding is used in the loss; (b) contrastive loss for slots $L_{contrastiveSF}(\phi)$ where the individual token embeddings are used in the loss. The regularized prototypical loss is the following:

$$L_{Total}(\phi) = \sum_{\mathbf{z} \in Q} \frac{1}{|Q|}\{L_{IC}(\phi, \mathbf{z}) + L_{Slots}(\phi, \mathbf{z})\} + \lambda_1 L_{contrastiveIC}(\phi) + \lambda_2 L_{contrastiveSF}(\phi) \tag{5}$$

We provide more details about the two contrastive losses in the Appendix section.

2.2 Data Augmentation for Few-shot IC/SF

Prior works in computer vision (Liu et al., 2020a; Ni et al., 2020) have shown that data augmentation

	Level	**SNIPS** (Kmax=20)		**ATIS** (Kmax=20)		**SNIPS** (Kmax=100)		**ATIS** (Kmax=100)	
		IC Acc	Slot F1	IC Acc	Slot F1	IC Acc	Slot F1	IC Acc	Slot F1
Krone et al. (2020)	-	0.877 ± 0.01	0.597 ± 0.017	0.660 ± 0.02	0.340 ± 0.004	0.877 ± 0.01	0.621 ± 0.007	0.719 ± 0.01	0.412 ± 0.02
Baseline (Ours)	-	0.887 ± 0.06	0.597 ± 0.04	0.737 ± 0.06	0.74 ± 0.01	0.907 ± 0.05	0.593 ± 0.04	0.80 ± 0.04	0.70± 0.02
CL (IC)	Support(m-train)	0.905 ± 0.05	0.594 ± 0.04	0.75 ± 0.07	0.748 ± 0.02	0.912 ± 0.03	0.594 ± 0.04	0.802 ± 0.06	0.70 ± 0.02
CL (IC)	Support,Query(m-train)	0.908 ± 0.06	0.596 ± 0.04	**0.76 ± 0.04**	0.748 ± 0.02	0.93 ± 0.05	0.60 ± 0.03	0.829 ± 0.06	0.703 ± 0.03
CL (IC + SF)	Support(m-train)	0.903 ± 0.06	0.60± 0.04	0.757 ± 0.04	0.755 ± 0.02	0.92 ± 0.01	0.60 ± 0.04	0.826 ± 0.05	0.70 ± 0.03
CL (IC + SF)	Support,Query(m-train)	**0.91 ± 0.04**	**0.60 ± 0.03**	0.75 ± 0.07	**0.756 ± 0.02**	**0.93 ± 0.03**	**0.60 ± 0.04**	**0.833 ± 0.05**	**0.71 ± 0.02**
CL (IC + SF), DA (Slot list)	Support,Query(m-train)	**0.921± 0.037**	**0.619± 0.037**	**0.803 ± 0.069**	0.748 ± 0.019	0.923± 0.055	**0.619± 0.035**	0.821± 0.08	**0.73± 0.02**

Table 1: Few-shot classification accuracy with contrastive learning (CL) for prototypical networks. For CL (IC) only $L_{contrastiveIC}$ is used, whereas for CL (IC + SF), both $L_{contrastiveIC}$ and $L_{contrastiveSF}$ are used.

is very effective in meta-learning. In this section, we use various data augmentation strategies to improve the meta-learning pipeline for IC/SF tasks. Data augmentation for joint IC/SF tasks in NLU is particularly challenging as the augmentation is primarily possible at the level of intents. For intent level data augmentation, we use state-of-the-art techniques such as backtranslation (Xie et al., 2019) and EDA (Wei and Zou, 2019b) along with prototypical networks. We also introduce a novel data augmentation technique called `slot-list values` which effectively leverages the structure of joint IC/SF tasks. In particular, we investigate the effectiveness of these data augmentation techniques in the meta-learning pipeline at different levels such as: (a) support at meta-training; (b) support + query at meta-training; (c) support at meta-testing; (d) combination of those. We provide details about these augmentation methods below.

2.2.1 `Slot-List Values` Augmentation

In IC/SF datasets, certain slot types often can take on values specified in a finite list. For example, in the SNIPS dataset the slot type *facility* can take on values from the list *["smoking room", "spa", "indoor", "outdoor", "pool", "internet", "parking", "wifi"]* . Specific to the discrete slot filling task, (Shah et al., 2019) used such values to learn an additional attention module for improving SF. Such lists can be created from the training dataset and be used for data augmentation. We leverage such lists to create synthetic utterances by replacing the values of slot types in a given utterance with other values from the list: e.g. given an utterance "*Book a table at a pool bar*", we synthesize another utterance "*Book a table at a indoor bar*".

2.2.2 Augmentation by Backtranslation

Backtranslation is a technique of translating an utterance into an intermediate language and back to its original language using a neural machine translation model. Previous works (Edunov et al., 2018; Yu et al., 2018; Sennrich et al., 2015) showed that backtranslation is extremely effective as a data augmentation technique for NLP applications. In our paper in particular, we use a pre-trained `en-es` NMT model (Junczys-Dowmunt et al., 2018) for generating the augmented utterances. To ensure that the generated utterances are diverse, we follow the procedure in (Xie et al., 2019) in which we employ restricted sampling from the model output probability distribution instead of beam-search.

2.2.3 EDA Data Augmentation

Adding small perturbations to the training data via random insertion, deletion, swapping and synonym replacement is one simple technique to generate synthetic data for data augmentation. Previous work by (Wei and Zou, 2019a) showed that EDA achieves state-of-the-art results on text-classification tasks. In our work, we use EDA to generate synthetic data to perform data augmentation at different stages of meta-learning.

3 Experiments

Datasets: We use two well-known IC/SF benchmarks: SNIPS (Coucke et al., 2018) and ATIS (Hemphill et al., 1990). SNIPS is a more challenging dataset as it contains intents from diverse domains whereas the ATIS dataset contains intents from only the *Airline* domain.

Episode Construction: We follow the standard episode construction technique described in (Krone et al., 2020; Triantafillou et al., 2020) where the number of classes and the shots per class in each episode are sampled dynamically.

Few-shot Splits: For the SNIPS dataset, we use 4 intent classes for meta-training and 3 intent classes for meta-testing. Similar to (Krone et al., 2020), we do not form a development split for SNIPS as there are only 7 intent classes and the episode construction process requires at least 3 classes in each split. For the ATIS dataset, we first select intent classes with more than 15 examples, then use 5 intent classes for meta-training and 7 intent classes for meta-testing. The rest of the

	Level	SNIPS(Kmax=20)	ATIS (Kmax=20)	SNIPS (Kmax=100)	ATIS(Kmax=100)
		IC Acc	IC Acc	IC Acc	IC Acc
(Krone et al., 2020)	-	0.877 ± 0.01	0.660 ± 0.02	0.877 ± 0.01	0.719 ± 0.01
Baseline (Ours)	-	0.887 ± 0.06	0.737 ± 0.06	0.907 ± 0.05	0.80 ± 0.04
DA (Slot-list)	Support(m-train)	0.898 ± 0.061	0.735 ± 0.052	0.916 ± 0.055	0.810 ± 0.052
DA (Slot-list)	Support,Query(m-train)	0.919 ± 0.062	**0.800 ± 0.054**	0.917 ± 0.051	0.806 ± 0.066
DA (Slot-list)	Support(m-train, m-test)	0.905± 0.062	0.772 ± 0.044	0.922± 0.051	0.818± 0.056
DA (Slot-list)	Support(m-test)	**0.926 ± 0.038**	0.764 ± 0.073	**0.931 ± 0.037**	**0.840± 0.047**
DA (Backtranslation)	Support(m-train)	0.885 ± 0.03	0.77 ± 0.06	0.928 ± 0.029	0.79 ± 0.06
DA (Backtranslation)	Support(m-train, m-test)	0.881 ± 0.03	0.79 ± 0.05	**0.931 ± 0.030**	0.795 ± 0.06
DA (Backtranslation)	Support(m-test)	0.895 ± 0.036	0.71 ± 0.06	0.899 ± 0.06	0.77 ± 0.14
DA (EDA)	Support(m-train)	0.893 ± 0.062	0.787 ± 0.07	0.911 ± 0.04	0.805 ± 0.08
DA (EDA)	Support(m-train,m-test)	0.893 ± 0.047	0.761 ± 0.08	0.915 ± 0.04	0.808 ± 0.10
DA (EDA)	Support(m-test)	0.892 ± 0.047	0.731 ± 0.06	0.915 ± 0.05	0.78 ± 0.059

Table 2: Few-shot IC accuracy with Data Augmentation (DA) for prototypical networks; m-train refers to meta-training and m-test refers to meta-testing

classes are used as a development split. In (Krone et al., 2020), the intent classes for each split are *manually chosen*. This is not representative of realistic situations where the types of few-shot classes can vary considerably. To address this issue, we report our experiment results averaged over 5 seeds where in each run the intent classes for each split are randomly sampled. In each experiment run, we evaluate our results for 100 episodes sampled from the test-split. We refer to our re-implementation of (Krone et al., 2020) with this strategy as *Baseline*.

Contrastive Learning Helps IC/SF tasks: Table 1 shows the results of experiments adding contrastive losses as a regularizer to our baseline. Overall, we observe that across both SNIPS and ATIS datasets, using contrastive losses as a regularizer predominantly improves IC accuracy, while marginally improving SF F1 score. In particular, we notice that using contrastive losses as a regularizer with both the support and query during meta-training leads to the best performances.

Impact of Data Augmentation is Dependent on Stage of Application: Table 2 shows the results of adding data augmentation to the few-shot IC tasks. We find that the data augmentation techniques in general improve the performance of few-shot IC, depending on the stage in the meta-learning pipeline at which the data is augmented. More specifically, for SNIPS we notice up to 4% and 2% gain in IC accuracy for $Kmax = 20$ and $Kmax = 100$ respectively. With EDA, we find that augmentation during meta-training and meta-testing together leads to a noteworthy gain in few-shot IC performances across both SNIPS and ATIS. In comparison, backtranslation is effective in improving the few-shot IC performance for SNIPS, when the shots per class is higher such as in $Kmax = 100$. However for ATIS, we observe a significant gain in IC only for $Kmax = 20$.

Slot-list Values Augmentation at Meta-Testing Helps: We find that dictionary based augmentation techniques such as `slot-list values` generally show consistent gain in IC at all stages during meta-training and shots per class.

Combination of Contrastive Learning and Data Augmentation Helps IC/SF tasks: We find that the combination of contrastive losses and data augmentation via `slot-list values` outperforms models trained independently with only contrastive losses or data augmentation. We hypothesize that this is due to two independent effects working together in conjunction: (a) contrastive learning helps to create improved prototypes whereas (b) data augmentation helps mitigate meta-overfitting.

For SF, we find that data augmentation leads to only limited improvements when compared to IC (see Appendix C). We attribute this to the low shots per slot class, an artifact of the episodic sampling procedure (Krone et al., 2020), done per intent class in the joint IC/SF setting.

4 Conclusion

In this work, we systematically dissect meta-learning pipelines for few-shot IC/SF tasks and identify stages during meta-learning where contrastive learning and data augmentation can be effective. Empirically, we found that contrastive losses are effective regularizers during meta-training and outperform the current state-of-the-art few-shot joint IC/SF benchmarks across both SNIPS and ATIS. Impact of data augmentation in general is highly dependent on the stage at which it is applied during meta-learning. Notably, a combination of contrastive losses and data augmentation via `slot-list values` during meta-training leads to the best performances across both SNIPS and ATIS. These strategies for improving few-shot IC/SF tasks create a strong benchmark and open up possibilities on more stronger modes of meta-specific augmentation and contrastive learning.

References

Ting Chen, Simon Kornblith, Mohammad Norouzi, and Geoffrey Hinton. 2020. A simple framework for contrastive learning of visual representations.

Alice Coucke, Alaa Saade, Adrien Ball, Théodore Bluche, Alexandre Caulier, David Leroy, Clément Doumouro, Thibault Gisselbrecht, Francesco Caltagirone, Thibaut Lavril, Maël Primet, and Joseph Dureau. 2018. Snips voice platform: an embedded spoken language understanding system for private-by-design voice interfaces.

Sergey Edunov, Myle Ott, Michael Auli, and David Grangier. 2018. Understanding back-translation at scale. *CoRR*, abs/1808.09381.

Steven Y. Feng, Varun Gangal, Jason Wei, Sarath Chandar, Soroush Vosoughi, Teruko Mitamura, and Eduard Hovy. 2021. A survey of data augmentation approaches for nlp.

Chelsea Finn, Pieter Abbeel, and Sergey Levine. 2017. Model-agnostic meta-learning for fast adaptation of deep networks. In *Proceedings of the 34th International Conference on Machine Learning*, volume 70 of *Proceedings of Machine Learning Research*, pages 1126–1135. PMLR.

Mauajama Firdaus, Shobhit Bhatnagar, Asif Ekbal, and Pushpak Bhattacharyya. 2018. A deep learning based multi-task ensemble model for intent detection and slot filling in spoken language understanding. In *Neural Information Processing*, pages 647–658, Cham. Springer International Publishing.

Ruiying Geng, Binhua Li, Yongbin Li, Jian Sun, and Xiaodan Zhu. 2020. Dynamic memory induction networks for few-shot text classification. In *Proceedings of the 58th Annual Meeting of the Association for Computational Linguistics*, pages 1087–1094, Online. Association for Computational Linguistics.

Ruiying Geng, Binhua Li, Yongbin Li, Yuxiao Ye, Ping Jian, and Jian Sun. 2019. Few-shot text classification with induction network. *CoRR*, abs/1902.10482.

Charles T. Hemphill, John J. Godfrey, and George R. Doddington. 1990. The ATIS spoken language systems pilot corpus. In *Speech and Natural Language: Proceedings of a Workshop Held at Hidden Valley, Pennsylvania, June 24-27,1990.*

Ganesh Jawahar, Benoît Sagot, and Djamé Seddah. 2019. What does BERT learn about the structure of language? In *Proceedings of the 57th Annual Meeting of the Association for Computational Linguistics*, pages 3651–3657, Florence, Italy. Association for Computational Linguistics.

Marcin Junczys-Dowmunt, Roman Grundkiewicz, Tomasz Dwojak, Hieu Hoang, Kenneth Heafield, Tom Neckermann, Frank Seide, Ulrich Germann, Alham Fikri Aji, Nikolay Bogoychev, André F. T. Martins, and Alexandra Birch. 2018. Marian: Fast neural machine translation in C++. In *Proceedings of ACL 2018, System Demonstrations*, pages 116–121, Melbourne, Australia. Association for Computational Linguistics.

Prannay Khosla, Piotr Teterwak, Chen Wang, Aaron Sarna, Yonglong Tian, Phillip Isola, Aaron Maschinot, Ce Liu, and Dilip Krishnan. 2020. Supervised contrastive learning. *CoRR*, abs/2004.11362.

Jason Krone, Yi Zhang, and Mona Diab. 2020. Learning to classify intents and slot labels given a handful of examples.

Kenton Lee, Kelvin Guu, Luheng He, Tim Dozat, and Hyung Won Chung. 2021. Neural data augmentation via example extrapolation.

Shiyang Li, Semih Yavuz, Kazuma Hashimoto, Jia Li, Tong Niu, Nazneen Rajani, Xifeng Yan, Yingbo Zhou, and Caiming Xiong. 2021. Coco: Controllable counterfactuals for evaluating dialogue state trackers.

Jialin Liu, Fei Chao, and Chih-Min Lin. 2020a. Task augmentation by rotating for meta-learning.

Zihan Liu, Genta Indra Winata, Peng Xu, and Pascale Fung. 2020b. Coach: A coarse-to-fine approach for cross-domain slot filling. *CoRR*, abs/2004.11727.

Renkun Ni, Micah Goldblum, Amr Sharaf, Kezhi Kong, and Tom Goldstein. 2020. Data augmentation for meta-learning.

Janarthanan Rajendran, Alex Irpan, and Eric Jang. 2020. Meta-learning requires meta-augmentation.

F. Ren and S. Xue. 2020. Intention detection based on siamese neural network with triplet loss. *IEEE Access*, 8:82242–82254.

Rico Sennrich, Barry Haddow, and Alexandra Birch. 2015. Improving neural machine translation models with monolingual data. *CoRR*, abs/1511.06709.

Darsh J. Shah, Raghav Gupta, Amir A. Fayazi, and Dilek Hakkani-Tür. 2019. Robust zero-shot cross-domain slot filling with example values. *CoRR*, abs/1906.06870.

Jake Snell, Kevin Swersky, and Richard S. Zemel. 2017. Prototypical networks for few-shot learning. *CoRR*, abs/1703.05175.

Dhanasekar Sundararaman, Vivek Subramanian, Guoyin Wang, Shijing Si, Dinghan Shen, Dong Wang, and Lawrence Carin. 2019. Syntax-infused transformer and BERT models for machine translation and natural language understanding. *CoRR*, abs/1911.06156.

Eleni Triantafillou, Tyler Zhu, Vincent Dumoulin, Pascal Lamblin, Utku Evci, Kelvin Xu, Ross Goroshin, Carles Gelada, Kevin Swersky, Pierre-Antoine Manzagol, and Hugo Larochelle. 2020. Meta-dataset: A dataset of datasets for learning to learn from few examples.

Jixuan Wang, Kai Wei, Martin Radfar, Weiwei Zhang, and Clement Chung. 2020. Encoding syntactic knowledge in transformer encoder for intent detection and slot filling.

Jason Wei and Kai Zou. 2019a. Eda: Easy data augmentation techniques for boosting performance on text classification tasks.

Jason W. Wei and Kai Zou. 2019b. EDA: easy data augmentation techniques for boosting performance on text classification tasks. *CoRR*, abs/1901.11196.

Qizhe Xie, Zihang Dai, Eduard H. Hovy, Minh-Thang Luong, and Quoc V. Le. 2019. Unsupervised data augmentation. *CoRR*, abs/1904.12848.

Wenxiu Xie, Dongfa Gao, Ruoyao Ding, and Tianyong Hao. 2018. A feature-enriched method for user intent classification by leveraging semantic tag expansion. In *Natural Language Processing and Chinese Computing*, pages 224–234, Cham. Springer International Publishing.

Adams Wei Yu, David Dohan, Minh-Thang Luong, Rui Zhao, Kai Chen, Mohammad Norouzi, and Quoc V. Le. 2018. Qanet: Combining local convolution with global self-attention for reading comprehension. *CoRR*, abs/1804.09541.

Chenwei Zhang, Wei Fan, Nan Du, and Philip S. Yu. 2016. Mining user intentions from medical queries: A neural network based heterogeneous jointly modeling approach. In *Proceedings of the 25th International Conference on World Wide Web*, WWW '16, page 1373–1384, Republic and Canton of Geneva, CHE. International World Wide Web Conferences Steering Committee.

A Hyperparameters

For the ATIS dataset, we use the development set to tune for λ_1 and λ_2 in Eq. (5). For the SNIPS dataset, we empirically set both λ_1 and λ_2 to be 0.06 due to the lack of a development set. In our experiments with the three data augmentation strategies, we generate synthetic utterances to exactly double the training data size for fair comparison throughout. Across all the experiments, we meta-train the models for 50 episodes and use a learning rate of $5e-5$.

B On Contrastive Learning

In our work, we use two types of contrastive losses for IC/SF tasks: (a) contrastive loss for intents $L_{contrastiveIC}(\phi)$ where the `<cls>` token embedding is used in the loss; (b) contrastive loss for slots $L_{contrastiveSF}(\phi)$ where the individual token embeddings from the encoder are used in the loss. In particular, we use the supervised contrastive loss (Khosla et al., 2020) and leverage the label information present in the support or support + query set during meta-training. First we define the contrastive loss for intents $L_{contrastiveIC}(\phi)$: given a set of utterances with their corresponding intent labels $S_{intents} = \{(x_i, y_i)_{i=1}^{m}\}$, assume $P(i)$ to be a set consisting of examples from $S_{intents}$ with same labels as the ith example. Formally $P(i) : \{x_j : y_j = y_i \ \forall j \in [1, m] \ \& \ j \neq i\}$. The contrastive loss for the intents $L_{contrastiveIC}(\phi)$ is defined as the following:

$$\sum_{i=1}^{m} -\log\left\{\frac{1}{|P(i)|}\sum_{z\in P(i)} \frac{\exp(f_\phi(x_i)^T f_\phi(z))/\tau}{\sum_{j=1,j\neq i}^{m}\exp(f_\phi(x_i)^T f_\phi(x_j))/\tau}\right\} \tag{6}$$

Here $f_\phi(x_i)$ denotes the `<cls>` embedding for the ith utterance. In case of slots, we first obtain the individual token embeddings in each utterance $x_i \ \forall i \in [1, m]$. Consider the total number of tokens to be N in an episode and their associated embeddings' set to be $S_{slots} = \{(h_j, y_j^{'}), \ \forall j \in N\}$, where $y_j^{'}$ is the slot label for the jth token. Similar to the intents, we define the set $Q(i) : \{h_j : y_j^{'} = y_i^{'} \ \forall j \in [1, N] \ \& \ j \neq i\}$. Next we define the contrastive loss for the slots $L_{slots}(\phi)$ as:

$$\sum_{i=1}^{N} -\log\left\{\frac{1}{|Q(i)|}\sum_{z\in Q(i)} \frac{\exp(h_i^T z)/\tau}{\sum_{j=1,j\neq i}^{N}\exp(h_i^T h_j)/\tau}\right\} \tag{7}$$

C Impact of Data Augmentation for Slot Filling

Data augmentation for joint IC/SF tasks is challenging as augmentation is only possible at the level of intents. Although data augmentation leads to large improvements in few-shot IC performances, its impact on SF tasks is limited. From Table 3, across the different data augmentation methods such as backtranslation, EDA and `slot-list values`, we observe that there is no consistent improvements in SF performances across our different experiment settings. We hypothesize that as data augmentation does not provide any direct signal to the SF task, the improvements are insubstantial. To address this issue and provide a more direct signal to the SF task, we incorporate part-of-speech (POS) and noun-phrase information of the different slot values into the joint IC/SF model. In the next section, we discuss ways to incorporate these additional syntactic information into the meta-learning pipeline.

D Beyond Semantic Information

Part-of-speech (POS) and noun-parser information can provide additional syntactic information about of an utterance, thus augmenting the semantic information from the encoded tokens. In particular, POS tags can help resolve decisions for ambiguous tokens or words. Previous work (Wang et al., 2020) has shown that prior information from POS tags helps in improving IC and SF tasks in the general supervised many shot setting. In our work, we use POS tags as an additional source of information particularly for the few-shot setting. We propose two primary ways to incorporate POS tags in the general meta-learning setting: (a) POS tag as an additional input feature; (b) Explicitly training the model to predict POS tags via a multi-task loss.

In addition to POS tags, we also augment information about noun-phrases as an additional input feature. Noun chunks or phrases have the potential to provide strong signals about possible spans of different slots to the underlying model, thus improving SF performance. For example, in the utterance "*book me a table for one at blue ribbon barbecue*"(with intent *BookRestaurant*, and slots: *party_size_number:"one", restaurant_name: "blue ribbon barbecue"*), *"blue ribbon barbecue"* is identified as a noun-chunk and the span information

	Level	SNIPS(Kmax=20)	ATIS (Kmax=20)	SNIPS (Kmax=100)	ATIS(Kmax=100)
		Slot F1	Slot F1	Slot F1	Slot F1
Baseline (Ours)	-	0.599 ± 0.04	0.748 ± 0.01	0.593 ± 0.04	0.703 ± 0.02
DA (Slot-list)	Support(m-train)	0.603 ± 0.043	0.738 ± 0.020	0.609 ± 0.047	0.713 ± 0.025
DA (Slot-list)	Support,Query(m-train)	**0.609 ± 0.043**	0.74 ± 0.02	0.609 ± 0.03	0.715 ± 0.02
DA (Slot-list)	Support(m-train, m-test)	0.587± 0.045	0.712 ± 0.026	0.595 ± 0.042	0.686± 0.029
DA (Slot-list)	Support(m-test)	0.572 ± 0.036	0.697 ± 0.028	0.589 ± 0.042	0.684± 0.02
DA (Backtranslation)	Support(m-train)	0.595 ± 0.04	0.742 ± 0.01	**0.611 ± 0.036**	**0.716 ± 0.02**
DA (Backtranslation)	Support(m-train, m-test)	0.595 ± 0.04	0.742 ± 0.01	**0.611 ± 0.03**	0.716 ± 0.02
DA(Backtranslation)	Support(m-test)	0.598 ± 0.03	0.74 ± 0.01	0.60 ± 0.03	0.72 ± 0.01
DA(EDA)	Support(m-train)	0.585 ± 0.032	0.742 ± 0.02	0.596 ± 0.05	0.701 ± 0.03
DA(EDA)	Support(m-train,m-test)	0.593 ± 0.033	0.742 ± 0.02	0.594 ± 0.04	0.711 ± 0.005
DA(EDA)	Support(m-test)	0.586 ± 0.036	0.74 ± 0.01	0.593 ± 0.037	**0.714 ± 0.02**

Table 3: Few-shot Slot F1 with Data Augmentation (DA) for prototypical networks; m-train refers to meta-training and m-test refers to meta-testing

	SNIPS (Kmax = 20)		SNIPS(Kmax=100)		ATIS(Kmax=20)		ATIS(Kmax=100)	
	IC Acc	Slot F1	IC Acc	Slot F1	IC Acc	Slot F1	IC Acc	Slot F1
Baseline (Ours)	0.887 ± 0.06	0.597 ± 0.04	0.907 ± 0.05	0.593 ± 0.04	0.737 ± 0.06	0.748 ± 0.02	0.801 ± 0.05	0.703 ± 0.02
Multi-task POS loss	0.905 ± 0.04	**0.603 ± 0.03**	**0.929 ± 0.03**	0.595 ± 0.03	**0.769 ± 0.06**	0.75 ± 0.01	0.807 ± 0.05	0.711 ± 0.02
With POS-tag features	0.896 ± 0.06	0.592 ± 0.04	0.926 ± 0.03	0.590 ± 0.04	0.745 ± 0.06	0.747 ± 0.01	0.793 ± 0.09	0.713 ± 0.02
With noun-parser features	**0.912 ± 0.05**	0.599 ± 0.04	0.897 ± 0.05	**0.597 ± 0.03**	0.764 ± 0.04	**0.755 ± 0.02**	0.805 ± 0.07	**0.715 ± 0.02**

Table 4: Effect of adding syntactic information into the joint IC/SF model

can potentially help with the SF task for the *restaurant_name* slot. Conversely, the POS tag for "*one*" is *NUM* and can help classify numeric words to the numeric slot *party_size_number*.

D.1 Feature-Based Addition

Previous works have shown that adding POS tags as features improves IC (Zhang et al., 2016; Xie et al., 2018) as well SF performances (Firdaus et al., 2018) in many-shot settings. In this work we look into incorporating syntactic features in our meta-learning pipeline. A simple idea to incorporate POS or noun-chunk tags of an utterance is to concatenate a vector representation of them, p_j^i and η_j^i respectively, with the token embeddings $f_\phi(x_j^i)$. Formally, in our meta-learning pipeline, we revise Eq. (2) for our slot prototype:

$$c_a = \frac{1}{|S_a|} \sum_{x_j^i \in S_a} f_\phi(x_j^i) \oplus p_j^i \oplus \eta_j^i \quad \forall x^i \in S \quad (8)$$

D.2 Multi-task POS Loss

Although training language models distills implicitly the structural knowledge of the underlying languages (Jawahar et al., 2019; Sundararaman et al., 2019) into the model, such knowledge can be imperfect. Explicitly training to learn structural knowledge such as POS tags (Wang et al., 2020), however, can help the model to improve on downstream tasks such as IC/SF. We treat POS tagging as a token level classification problem, similar to SF. Given a support set S, assume S_l to consist of utterances belonging to the intent class c_l, S_a to consist of tokens from the slot class c_a and S_{pos} to consist of POS tag tokens from the class c_{pos}. In addition to the intent class prototypes c_l and slot class prototypes c_a, we define an additional class prototype c_{pos} for the POS tags:

$$c_{pos} = \frac{1}{|S_{pos}|} \sum_{x_j^i \in S_{pos}} f_\phi(x_j^i) \quad \forall x^i \in S \quad (9)$$

Given a query example **z**, we define the corresponding loss with the POS tag prototypes as:

$$L_{pos}(\phi, \mathbf{z}) = -\log\{\frac{\exp(-d(f_\phi(\mathbf{z}), c_{pos}))}{\sum_{pos'} \exp(-d(f_\phi(\mathbf{z}), c_{pos'}))}\} \quad (10)$$

For the query set Q, the composite loss function is the following:

$$L_{Total}(\phi) = \sum_{\mathbf{z} \in Q} \frac{1}{|Q|}\{L_{IC}(\phi, \mathbf{z}) + L_{Slots}(\phi, \mathbf{z}) + \beta L_{pos}(\phi, \mathbf{z})\} \quad (11)$$

where β is a hyperparameter. For the ATIS dataset, we select β by using a validation set. In case of the SNIPS dataset, we empirically set β as 0.01 due to unavailability of a development set.

In Table 4, we observe an improvement in both IC and SF over the baseline with the addition of information from the POS tags as an auxiliary loss.

However, similar to feature-based addition, we notice only a marginal and small improvement for SF. To understand further this issue, we exmined the episodic sampling procedure used in (Krone et al., 2020). Across both the SNIPS and ATIS datasets, the average shots per class for intents are ≈ 5 and ≈ 10 for $Kmax = 20$ and $Kmax = 100$ respectively. However for slots, we find that the average shots per class are ≈ 1.3 and ≈ 3 for $Kmax = 20$ and $Kmax = 100$ respectively. We conjecture that as the shots per class for slots are much lesser in comparison to that of intents, it results in smaller improvements when compared to intents in the joint IC/SF setting.

E Compute

For all our experiments we primarily use a V100-16GB GPU. For meta-training on ATIS for $Kmax = 100$ with data augmentation, we use V100-32GB GPU due to increased memory requirements.

F Note on Data Augmentation Techniques

In our paper, we investigate only a limited number of data augmentation techniques specific to natural language processing. We note that in the recent years, a wide variety of augmentation techniques for NLP has been developed (See (Feng et al., 2021) for a good overview). However, we choose EDA, backtranslation and use a dictionary based `slot-list values` in our experiments due to it's inherent simplicity which can enable easy integration with existing meta-learning methods. Designing and adapting existing augmentation techniques to meta-learning is a future direction of research.

Learning Open Domain Multi-hop Search Using Reinforcement Learning

Enrique Noriega-Atala
The University of Arizona
enoriega@arizona.edu

Mihai Surdeanu
The University of Arizona
msurdeanu@arizona.edu

Clayton T. Morrison
The University of Arizona
claytonm@arizona.edu

Abstract

We propose a method to teach an automated agent to *learn how to search* for multi-hop paths of relations between entities in an open domain. The method learns a policy for directing existing information retrieval and machine reading resources to focus on relevant regions of a corpus. The approach formulates the learning problem as a Markov decision process with a state representation that encodes the dynamics of the search process and a reward structure that minimizes the number of documents that must be processed while still finding multi-hop paths. We implement the method in an actor-critic reinforcement learning algorithm and evaluate it on a dataset of search problems derived from a subset of English Wikipedia. The algorithm finds a family of policies that succeeds in extracting the desired information while processing fewer documents compared to several baseline heuristic algorithms.

1 Introduction

The sheer size of public corpora such as Wikipedia[1] or large paper repositories like arXiv[2] and PubMed Central[3] poses an enormous challenge to automating effective search for relevant information. This problem is compounded when the underlying information needs require *multi-hop connections*, e.g., searching for biological mechanisms that connect two proteins (Cohen, 2015) or searching for explanations that require complex reasoning by understanding text supported by different documents in QA systems (Welbl et al., 2018; Yang et al., 2018).

In a naive approach, an automated information extraction agent could process all the documents in a corpus, searching for the indirect connections that satisfy a multi-hop information need. However, this quickly becomes prohibitively expensive as the corpus size increases. Further, the documents may also be behind a paywall, adding an additional economic cost to accessing information. Thus, the naive exhaustive reading approach is simply not feasible for most large corpora scenarios. Instead, we need to incorporate the kind of iterative *focused reading* that humans are capable of. When people search for information, they use background knowledge, based in part on what they have just read, to narrow down the search space while selectively committing time and other resources to carefully reading documents that appear relevant. This process may be repeated multiple times until the information need is satisfied.

We propose a methodology that uses reinforcement learning (RL) to teach an automated agent how to direct a search process, using existing information retrieval and machine learning components selectively, focusing on the relevant parts of the corpus in order to minimize the expenditure of computational resources and access costs.

The contributions of our work are the following:

1. A reinforcement learning framework to teach an automated agent how to direct a multi-hop search process that selectively allocates machine reading resources in an open-domain corpus.

2. A set of domain-agnostic state representation features that enable the reinforcement learning method to learn a policy that improves the chances of finding the desired information while processing fewer documents compared to strong baselines.

3. A new dataset of open-domain multi-hop search problems derived from English Wikipedia contained in the WikiHop dataset [4] (Welbl et al., 2018). Using this dataset, we show that our RL approach is able

[1] https://www.wikipedia.org/
[2] http://arxiv.org/
[3] https://www.ncbi.nlm.nih.gov/pmc/
[4] http://qangaroo.cs.ucl.ac.uk

Proceedings of the Workshop on Structured and Unstructured Knowledge Integration (SUKI), pages 26 - 35
July 14, 2022 ©2022 Association for Computational Linguistics

to derive policies that find the desired information more frequently and by processing fewer documents than several heuristic baselines.

2 Related Work

Modern machine reading technology enables the extraction of structured information from natural language data. Named-entity recognition (Tjong Kim Sang and De Meulder, 2003) systems detect and label specific classes of concepts from text, both in the general domain (Manning et al., 2014) and for specific domains (Neumann et al., 2019). Relation extraction systems extract interactions between different concepts in open-domain (DBL, 2018, 2017, 2008) and domain-specific scenarios (Jin-Dong et al., 2019; Demner-Fushman et al., 2019; Cohen et al., 2011).

Reinforcement learning has been successfully deployed for a variety of natural language processing (NLP) tasks. (Clark and Manning, 2016) proposed a policy-gradient method to resolve the correct coreference chains for the task of coreference resolution. (Li et al., 2017) used reinforcement learning to train an end-to-end task-completion dialogue system. For the task of machine translation, (He et al., 2016) formulated the task as a dual-learning game in which two agents teach each other without the need of human labelers using policy-gradient algorithms.

Reinforcement learning has also been specifically applied to improving search and machine reading. In learning how to search, (Kanani and McCallum, 2012) proposed a methodology for the task of slot-filling based on temporal-difference q-learning that uses domain specific state representation features to select actions in a resource-constrained scenario. (Noriega-Atala et al., 2017) successfully applied RL to finding relevant biochemical interactions in a large corpus by focusing the allocation of machine reading resources towards the most promising documents. Similarly, (Wang et al., 2019) explore the use of deep neural networks and deep RL to simulate the search behavior of a researcher, also in the biomedical domain.

3 Learning to Search

We propose a methodology to teach an automated agent how to selectively retrieve and read documents in an iterative fashion in order to *efficiently* find multi-hop connections between a pair of concepts (or entities). Each search step focuses on a restricted set of documents that are hypothesized to be more relevant for finding a connection between the two target concepts. The focus set is retrieved and processed and if a path connecting the concepts is found, the search terminates. Otherwise, a new set of focus documents is identified based on what has been learned so far during the search. The process is repeated iteratively until the desired information is found or a number of iterations is exceeded. Our method is general as it does not directly rely on any supervised domain specific semantics.

During the search, the agent iteratively constructs a *knowledge graph* (KG) that represents the relations between concepts found so far through machine reading. In each iteration, the algorithm formulates a document retrieval query based on the current state of the knowledge graph, which is then executed by an information retrieval (IR) component. The IR component contains data structures to query the corpus, for example using an inverted index. The construction of these data structures usually only requires shallow processing, such as tokenization and stemming, and not a full-fledged NLP pipeline. Any documents returned from executing the query are processed by an information extraction (IE) component that performs named entity recognition and relation extraction. The KG is expanded by adding newly identified entities as new nodes and previously unseen relations as new edges. The overall goal of the method is to focus on the documents that appear to be most likely to contain a path between the target concepts, all while processing as few documents as possible.

(Noriega-Atala et al., 2017) formalized this iterative search process as a family of *focused reading* algorithms, shown in Algorithm 1:

Algorithm 1 Focused reading algorithm

```
procedure FocusedReading(E1, E2)
    KG ← {{E1, E2}, ∅}
    repeat
        Q ← BuildQuery(KG)
        (V, E) ← Retrieval+Extraction(Q)
        Expand(V, E, KG)
    until IsConnected(E1, E2) OR HasTimedOut
end procedure
```

The algorithm starts with the KG representing only the *endpoints* of the search: the named entities $E1$ and $E2$. The algorithm then initiates the search loop. The first step in the loop analyzes the knowledge graph and generates an information retrieval query, Q. As we will describe shortly, the current state of the KG is used to parameterize and constrain the scope of Q, focusing it on returning a limited subset of documents that are hypothesized to be most relevant. After retrieval, the documents are processed by the IE component. Any entities not previously found in the KG are placed in the new entity set V, and similarly any new relations linking entities are placed in the new relation set, E. V and E are incorporated into the KG and the algorithm then searches the updated KG for any new possible paths connecting $E1$ and $E2$. If a path exists, it is returned as a candidate explanation of how $E1$ and $E2$ are related. Otherwise, if no such path exists, the query formulation process (using the updated KG) followed by IR and IE, is repeated until a path is found or the process times out.

This framework can answer multi-hop search queries for which the relationships along a connecting path come from different documents. For example, this process may discover that *Valley of Mexico* is connected to the *Aztecs* because the Aztecs were a *pre-columbian civilization* (found in one document), which, in turn, was located in the Valley of Mexico (found in another document).

In the following subsections, we formulate focused reading as a Markov decision process (MDP).

3.1 Constructing Query Actions

Template	***# Params***	***Constraints***
Conjunction	Two: (A, B)	Contains A and B
Singleton	One: (E)	Contains E
Disjunction	Two: (A, B)	Contains A or B

Table 1: Query templates

In the focused reading MDP, actions are comprised of information retrieval queries. Actions are constructed from a set of three *query templates*, listed in Table 1. Each template is parameterized by one or two arguments representing the entities that are the subject of the query. The template type then incorporates these entities into the set of constraints that must be satisfied by a document in order to be retrieved. The different query templates are intuitively designed to give the agent the choice of either *exploring* the corpus by performing a broader search through the more permissive disjunctive query (documents are retrieved if either of the entities are present), or instead *exploiting* particular regions of the corpus through the more restrictive conjunctive query (the documents must contain both entities).

Because *conjunctive* queries return documents with the text of both entities, they are more likely to identify relations connecting the entities. However, there is also an increased risk that such queries will end up not finding any satisfying documents, especially when the entities are not closely related, resulting in waisting one iteration in the search process. On the other hand, *disjunctive* queries are designed to return a larger set of documents, which, reduce the likelihood of returning an empty set. But they introduce the risk of processing more potentially irrelevant documents, and potentially introducing more irrelevant entities. *Singleton* queries represent a compromise between conjunction and disjunction. They are designed to expand the set of existing queries to the knowledge graph, which may in turn be along paths that connect the target entities, but retrieving documents related to just one entity, rather than two.

Every entity or pair of entities in the current knowledge graph is eligible to serve as a parameter in a query template. The challenge is to choose which entities paired with query template type are more likely to retrieve documents containing candidate paths, using only the domain-agnostic information present in the KG.

As the search process proceeds, the number of entities in the knowledge graph grows, in turn increasing the number of possible query actions that can be constructed. RL quickly becomes intractable as the state and action space grows. We therefore perform a beam search to fix the cardinality of the action space to a constant size. In particular, we use cosine similarity (for entity pairs) and average tf-idf scores (for single entities) to rank the entities that might participate in constructing query actions. The agent then chooses among the top n entities/pairs for each query template, thus bounding the total number of actions available to the agent to $3n$ different queries at each step.

We rank candidate entity pairs that might participate in query templates involving two entities by computing the cosine similarity of the vector representations of the entities. We use the natural language expression representation of the named entities to construct a continuous vector representation. The vector representation of each entity is built by averaging the word embedding vectors[5] of the words in the text of the named entity description. This similarity works as a proxy indicator of how related those entities are, under the intuition that entities that have similar embeddings are more likely to participate in relations.

For singleton entity queries, we use the average tf-idf score of the entity's natural language description for ranking. The tf-idf score of an entity is derived from averaging the tf-idf score of the individual terms in the entity's natural language description. Each term's frequency value is based on the *complete corpus*. Tf-idf scores are often used as a proxy measure of term importance (the term occurs selectively with greater frequency within some documents), so here the intuition is that entities with higher tf-idf scores may be associated with higher recall in the corpus.

Finally, there is an additional non-query action that is available in every step of the search: *early stop*. If the agent choses to stop early, the search process transitions to a final, unsuccessful state. This deprives the agent from successfully finding a path, but avoids incurring further cost of processing more documents in a possibly unfruitful search.

3.2 State Representation Features

At each step during search, the focused reading agent will select just one action to execute (a query action or early stop) based on the current search state. The agent makes this decision using a model that estimates for each action the expected long-term reward that can be achieved by taking that action in the current state. Here we describe the collection of features used to represent the current state, provided as input to the model.

Table 2 provides a summary of the features included in the state representation. We group them into four categories.

- *Search state features*: Information about the current state of the search process including: the number of documents that have been processed so far; how long has the search been running (expressed in iterations); and the size of the knowledge graph.

- *Endpoints of the search*: $E1$ and $E2$ represent the original target concepts that we are trying to find a path between. The identity of the endpoints determines the starting point of the search and conditions the theme of the content sought during the search. This information is provided to the model using the vector embedding representations of $E1$ and $E2$.

Category	***Feature***
Search state	Iteration number Doc set size # of vertices in KG # of edges
Endpoints	Embedding of $E1$ Embedding of $E2$
Query	Cosine sim. or avg tf-idf score # of new documents to add
Topic Modeling	Δ Entropy of queries KL Divergence of query

Table 2: State representation features

- *Query features*: We include in the state representation features the score with which each of the $3n$ queries in the action space is ranked. This includes the cosine similarity for conjunction and disjunction queries and tf-idf score for singleton queries. The intuition is that the score may be correlated with the expected long-term reward. For each query action, we will also see the identities of which documents will be retrieved. This allows us to count how many documents will be retrieved that have not already contributed to the KG, and this is included in the state representation for each action.

- *Topic modeling features*: Finally, we would like to incorporate some indication of what information is contained in the documents that might be retrieved, and how it relates to the current entities within the KG. As a proxy for this information, we model the topics in the potentially retrieved documents, by peeking into the IR component to see the identity of documents that would be returned by the queries in the action space, and compare them to the topics represented in the KG using two numerical scores: (a) an approximation of how broad or specific the topics are in the set of documents that would be returned by the query, and (b) an estimate of how the knowledge graph's *topic distribution* would change if the query is selected as the next action.

[5]We used the pretrained GloVe model provided by spaCy at `https://spacy.io/models/en#en_core_web_lg`

3.3 Topic Modeling Features

Topic modeling features can be useful for staying *on topic* throughout the search, avoiding drift into potentially irrelevant content. Consider the following example: A user wants to know how the Red Sox and the Golden State Warriors are related by searching Wikipedia. While the two entities cover different sports in different regions of the United States, it is more likely that the connection will occur in a document about sports, e.g., they are both covered by the ESPN TV station.

We use Latent Dirichlet Allocation (Blei et al., 2003) (LDA) to provide the agent the ability to exploit topic information available in the corpus. LDA is unsupervised and requires only shallow processing of the corpus, namely, tokenizing and optionally stemming. This is essentially the same information required for constructing an inverted index for IR, so can be computed along with the IR component used in the focused reading system.

LDA produces a topic distribution for each document. We then aggregate the set of documents by summing the topic frequencies across documents and renormalizing. The topic distribution of the KG is then the aggregation of the topic distributions of the documents processed so far in the search process. The topic distribution of a query is the aggregation of the topic distributions of the *unseen* documents returned by the query.

We consider two statistics for relating topic distributions: topic entropy and Kullback-Leibler (KL) divergence.

Intuitively, the *entropy* of a topic distribution is an estimate of how *specialized* a document is, that is, how much it focuses on a particular set of topics. For example, a document that only talks about a specific sport will generally have a topic distribution where the mass is concentrated only on the particular topics of that sport, and therefore have a lower entropy than another document that discusses sports and business. Document sets with overall higher entropy are more likely to introduce information about more topics to the knowledge graph, and therefore produce more opportunities for new links between a broader set of entities. Lower entropy queries focus on a narrower set of topics, and thus, may introduce links between a restricted set of entities. The difference in entropy expresses this intuition in relative terms. We introduce a feature, Δ Entropy, as the difference in entropy between documents retrieved by a candidate action and the documents the action retrieved in the previous step. Positive values indicate that the candidate query will generally expand the topics compared to those fetched the last step while negative values indicate more restricted topic focus.

Δ Entropy measures how concentrated the mass is, but it does not tell us *how* the distributions are different. Two document sets may have completely different topic distributions, yet have the same or similar entropy. Kullback-Leibler (KL) divergence (Kullback and Leibler, 1951), also known as relative entropy, helps measure how different two distributions are with respect to each other, even if they have the same absolute entropy. To capture this information, we compute the KL divergence between the topic distribution in the new documents (retrieved by the new query) and the topic distribution of the knowledge graph. This estimates how different the information in the new query is relative to what has already been retrieved.

3.4 Reward Function Structure

The overall goal of the focused reading learning processes is to identify a policy that efficiently finds paths of relations between the target entities while minimizing the number of documents that must be processed by the IE component. To achieve this, we want the reward structure of the MDP to incorporate the tradeoff between the number of documents that have to be read (the reading cost) and whether the agent can successfully find a path between the entities. Equation 1 describes the reward function, where s_t represents the current state and a_t represents the action executed in that state.

$$r(s_t, a_t) = \begin{cases} S & \text{if } s_{t+1} \text{ is succesful sate} \\ -c \times m & \text{if } m > 0 \\ -e & \text{if } m = 0 \end{cases} \qquad (1)$$

A positive reward S (for "success") is given when executing a_t results in a transition to a state whose knowledge graph contains a path connecting the target entities. Otherwise, the search is not yet complete and the a cost is incurred for processing m documents with machine reading on step t. The cost is adjusted by a hyper parameter c that controls the relative expense of processing a single document. Note that there may be actions that return an empty document set, incurring no cost from reading, but still not making progress in the search. To discourage the agent from choosing such actions, the hyperparameter e controls the cost of executing an unfruitful action that returns no new information. (Specific parameter values used in this work are presented in Table 4 of Section 5.)

4 Evaluation and Discussion

To evaluate the focused reading learning method, we introduce a novel dataset derived from the English version of Wikipedia. Our dataset consist of a set of 369 multi-hop search problems, where a search problem is consists of a pair of entities to be connected by a path of relations, potentially connecting to other entities along the path.

The foundation of the dataset is a subset of 6,880 Wikipedia articles from the WikiHop (Welbl et al., 2018) corpus. We used Wikification (Ratinov et al., 2011; Cheng and Roth, 2013) to extract named entities from these documents and normalize them to the title of a corresponding Wikipedia article. Wikification does not perform relation extraction, so we lack gold-standard relations. To overcome this limitation, in this paper we induce a relation between entities that co-occur within a window of three sentences. Every relation extracted this way can be traced back to at least one document in the corpus.

We create a gold-standard knowledge graph using the induced entities and relations, and we sample pairs of entities connected by paths to create search problems for the dataset. Table 3 contains a break-down of the number of elements in each subset of the dataset.

Element	***Size***
Corpus	6880 articles
Search Problems	
Training	230 problems
Development	500 problems
Testing	670 problems
Total	1400 problems

Table 3: Multi-hop search dataset details.

We train an LDA model[6] and constructed an information retrieval inverted index over the collection of documents.[7]

We used the Advantage Actor Critic algorithm (Mnih et al., 2016) (A2C) to implement our reinforcement learning focused reading method.[8]

A2C is an actor-critic method and we use a single neural network architecture to model the action policy (actor) as well as the state value function (critic). We use a single neural network architecture to implement the A2C actor-critic model. The architecture consists of a fully-connected feed-forward neural network with four layers and two output *heads*. The first output head represents the approximation of the *action policy* (the actor) as a soft-max activation layer whose size is the cardinality of the action space. This approximates the probability distribution of the actions given the current state. The second head approximates the *state value*, as a single neuron with a linear activation. The state value estimates the expected long-term reward of using the estimated action distribution of the first head in the current state. Altogether the model consists of approximately 3.79 million parameters.

Table 4 lists the hyper-parameter values used in our experiments. [9]

Hyper-parameter	***Value***
Environment	
# entities per query template	15
Maximum # of steps	10
Reward Function	
Successful outcome S	1000
Document processing cost c	10
Empty query cost e	100
Training	
Mini-batch size	100
# Iterations	2000

Table 4: Hyper-parameter values

We performed an ablation analysis on the development dataset to find the best configuration of features.

The development dataset contains five hundred search problems. The set of endpoints of the search problems does not overlap with those of the training and validation datasets. This is enforced to avoid any accidental leak of training information.

Table 5 contains the results of the ablation experiments. All the search problems were repeated five times with different random seeds. The key columns of the table are defined as follows. *Success Rate* represents the percentage of problems in the test set for which the agent connected the endpoints.

[6]We used the LDA implementation provided by gensim `https://radimrehurek.com/gensim_3.8.3/`.

[7]Code and dataset files are found at `https://ml4ai.github.io/OpenDomainFR/`

[8]Implemented using the rlpyt library hosted at `https://github.com/astooke/rlpyt`.

[9]Hyper-parameter values were determined through manual tunning.

	Success Rate	Processed Documents	Documents per Success	Average Steps Overall	 Successes	 Failures
			Baselines			
Random	25.04 (0.014)	56,187.8 (3,197.6)	449.83 (34.34)	8.41 (0.06)	3.66 (0.25)	10 (0)
Conditional	23.92 (0.008)	49,609.8 (4,215.11)	415.03 (36.01)	8.51 (0.06)	3.78 (0.07)	10 (0)
Cascade	32.84 (0.01)	62,058.2 (3,686.57)	378.15 (23.87)	7.42 (0.05)	2.93 (0.19)	9.61 (0.06)
			All Features			
Dropout 0.2	36 (0.007)*	58,552.2 (719.67)*	325.41 (8.43)*	6.56 (0.05)	2.22 (0.06)	9.01 (0.04)
Dropout 0.5	36.64 (0.004)*	100,869 (4,121)	550.76 (26.2)	7 (0.04)	2.37 (0.08)	9.67 (0.06)
No Embs	26.3 (0.008)	**39,433 (1,678.2)***	428.82 (19.51)	6.52 (0.03)	2.37 (0.08)	7.74 (0.07)
			No Query Features			
Dropout 0.2	33.68 (0.003)	42,022.2 (2,071.89)*	**249.57 (13.02)***	4.56 (0.05)	2.02 (0.03)	5.84 (0.08)
Dropout 0.5	36.48 (0.003)*	62,126.6 (1,900.75)	340.62 (10.79)*	5.95 (0.06)	2.28 (0.03)	8.06 (0.09)
No Embs	35.6 (0.005)*	58,025.8 (1,085.72)*	325.99 (4.26)*	6.37 (0.07)	2.2 (0.07)	8.68 (0.12)
			No Search Features			
Dropout 0.2	35.92 (0.002)*	55,723 (1,437.01)*	310.27 (8.13)*	6.42 (0.04)	2.15 (0.03)	8.82 (0.07)
Dropout 0.5	35.32 (0.003)*	53,227.4 (1,429.88)*	301.42 (8.77)*	5.41 (0.07)	2.09 (0.02)	7.22 (0.11)
No Embs	**37.16 (0.004)***	97,612.2 (4,550.54)	525.48 (26.72)	6.92 (0)	2.44 (0.08)	9.56 (0.01)
			No Topic Features			
Dropout 0.2	**35.56 (0.004)***	**51,757.4 (1,510.95)***	**291.11 (8.36)***	*5.92 (0.02)*	**2.15 (0.07)**	**8 (0.05)**
Dropout 0.5	35.72 (0.007)*	55,637 (1,456.53)*	311.58 (8.74)*	5.56 (0.05)	2.13 (0.06)	7.46 (0.06)
No Embs	28.52 (0.004)	50,634.6 (2,060.88)*	355.05 (12.1)	6.74 (0.06)	3.5 (0.04)	8.03 (0.1)

Table 5: Feature sets ablation results. * denotes the difference w.r.t. the cascade baseline is statistically significant.

Processed Docs provides the number of documents processed in all the search problems of the test set. *Docs per Success* is a summary the other two columns: it contains the number of documents processed divided by the number of successes. This ratio is an aggregate statistic useful for comparing the performance between different policies. We report the sample averages and their standard deviations in parentheses. For example, the *Success Rate* column displays the average and standard deviation of five success rate calculations over five hundred search problems. The *Processed Documents* column displays the average and standard deviation of the cumulative count of documents processed in the search problems, and so forth.

We implement three baseline policies that were not derived using RL:

- *Random*: Uniformly randomly selects a query from all possible queries constructed from eligible combinations of entities assigned to the query templates.
- *Conditional Random*: Uniformly randomly selects a query template, *conjunction, disjunction* and *singleton* and then choses the uniformly randomly selects the entities to parameterize the template.
- *Cascade*: Uniformly randomly samples a pair of entities and executes a conjunction query. If the result set does not contain any documents, then the agent selects a disjunction query with the same entities.

For consistency, each baseline was also evaluated with five different random seeds over the testing set. The top part of Table 5 shows the results of the baseline policies.

To test for statistical significance, we performed a non-parametric bootstrap resampling test with ten thousand samples for the the following metrics: *success rate, processed documents* and *documents per success*. For each metric, we calculated the difference between the result of the cascade baseline and the result of each of the reinforcement learning (RL) policies. If $p \leq 0.05$ of the difference being in favor of the reinforcement learning policy, the quantity is starred in the table.

In terms of success rate, most of the reinforcement learning models perform better than the cascade baseline. The notable exceptions are two feature configurations that do not use endpoint embeddings. These configurations are the one that

	Success Rate	Processed Documents	Documents per Success	Average Steps Overall	Successes	Failures
			Baseline			
Cascade	36.52 (0.008)	83,252.4 (2,538.11)	339.39 (13.01)	7.18 (0.06)	2.81 (0.05)	9.69 (0.04)
			No Topic Features			
Dropout 0.2	39.02 (0.007)*	**79,737.2 (1,664.65)**	**304.22 (10.06)***	**6.28 (0.04)**	2.16 (0.08)	**8.91 (0.03)**
			All Features			
Dropout 0.2	**39.49 (0.003)***	85,637.8 (1,751.95)	322.71 (7.99)	6.34 (0.04)	**2.16 (0.03)**	9.07 (0.06)

Table 6: Results of the best model in the testing dataset. Quantities are averages over five runs with different random seeds and standard deviations are shown in parentheses. * denotes the difference w.r.t. the cascade baseline is statistically significant.

considers all feature classes and the one that does not consider topic features.

Excluding query features from training produces models that process fewer documents per success with or without endpoint embeddings.

Excluding search features produced in average models with higher success rate, with or without embeddings, but does so while processing more documents compared to other configurations.

The configurations that exclude query features produced models with the best numbers of documents per success. When the topic features are excluded, a similar result is achieved, but the number of documents per success of model that does not use endpoint embeddings is not statistically significantly lower than that of the cascade baseline.

Nonetheless the model that has the best balance between *success rate* and *documents per success* is the one that excludes topic features and trains with a dropout coefficient of 0.2 on the endpoint embeddings. We use this model to evaluate the validation dataset.

Table 6 displays the results of the cascade baseline, which shows the strongest performance among the baseline policies, and the chosen reinforcement learning model on the validation dataset. The validation dataset contains 650 search problems and the set of endpoints of its search problems is disjoint from the other datasets' for the same reason, to avoid leaking any training or development signal into the validation dataset. We did the same non-parametric bootstrap test for statistical significance. The reinforcement learning policy achieves approximately 2.5% higher average success rate on the testing dataset that the cascade baseline policy. While it also processes fewer documents in average, the difference is not statistically significant, but when considering the number of documents per success, the result is indeed significant, requiring approximately thirty five documents in average than cascade.

5 Conclusions

We proposed a focused reading methodology to automatically learn how to direct search in large corpora while iteratively building a knowledge base. The knowledge base is modeled as a graph, which in turn is used to focus the search toward documents that appear relevant. Our methodology complements existing information retrieval and machine tools. We evaluated focused reading on a set of search problems extracted from English Wikipedia and demonstrated that reinforcement learning with a state representation based on features about dynamics of the search process and the properties of the corpus is more effective and efficient than heuristic baselines. In this methodology, inference in a knowledge graph acquired during the search process is agnostic of the semantics of the concepts and their relations. Their quality depends on the machine reading components used to extract them.

In future work, we plan to explore approaches for incorporating the semantics of the relations along the multi-hop paths that connect the target entities. Crucially, this includes incorporating additional constraints based on topic context. Providing context to a search problem could prove useful to better focus the search process and to improve the accuracy of inference. We also plan to adapt the focused reading methodology to handle other class of search problems, e.g., slot filling tasks where the endpoints are underspecified.

References

2008. *Proceedings of the First Text Analysis Conference, TAC 2008, Gaithersburg, Maryland, USA, November 17-19, 2008*. NIST.

2017. *Proceedings of the 2017 Text Analysis Conference, TAC 2017, Gaithersburg, Maryland, USA, November 13-14, 2017*. NIST.

2018. *Proceedings of the 2018 Text Analysis Conference, TAC 2018, Gaithersburg, Maryland, USA, November 13-14, 2018*. NIST.

David Blei, Andrew Ng, and Michael I. Jordan. 2003. Latent dirichlet allocation. *Journal of Machine Learning Research*, 3:993–1022.

Xiao Cheng and Dan Roth. 2013. Relational inference for wikification. In *Proceedings of the 2013 Conference on Empirical Methods in Natural Language Processing*, pages 1787–1796, Seattle, Washington, USA. Association for Computational Linguistics.

Kevin Clark and Christopher D. Manning. 2016. Improving coreference resolution by learning entity-level distributed representations. In *Proceedings of the 54th Annual Meeting of the Association for Computational Linguistics (Volume 1: Long Papers)*, pages 643–653, Berlin, Germany. Association for Computational Linguistics.

Kevin Bretonnel Cohen, Dina Demner-Fushman, Sophia Ananiadou, John Pestian, Jun'ichi Tsujii, and Bonnie Webber, editors. 2011. *Proceedings of BioNLP 2011 Workshop*. Association for Computational Linguistics, Portland, Oregon, USA.

Paul R Cohen. 2015. Darpa's big mechanism program. *Physical biology*, 12(4):045008.

Dina Demner-Fushman, Kevin Bretonnel Cohen, Sophia Ananiadou, and Junichi Tsujii, editors. 2019. *Proceedings of the 18th BioNLP Workshop and Shared Task*. Association for Computational Linguistics, Florence, Italy.

Di He, Yingce Xia, Tao Qin, Liwei Wang, Nenghai Yu, Tie-Yan Liu, and Wei-Ying Ma. 2016. Dual learning for machine translation. In *Advances in neural information processing systems*, pages 820–828.

Kim Jin-Dong, Nédellec Claire, Bossy Robert, and Deléger Louise, editors. 2019. *Proceedings of The 5th Workshop on BioNLP Open Shared Tasks*. Association for Computational Linguistics, Hong Kong, China.

Pallika H. Kanani and Andrew K. McCallum. 2012. Selecting actions for resource-bounded information extraction using reinforcement learning. In *Proceedings of the fifth ACM international conference on Web search and data mining*, pages 253–262.

Solomon Kullback and Richard A. Leibler. 1951. On information and sufficiency. *The annals of mathematical statistics*, 22(1):79–86.

Xiujun Li, Yun-Nung Chen, Lihong Li, Jianfeng Gao, and Asli Celikyilmaz. 2017. End-to-end task-completion neural dialogue systems. In *Proceedings of the Eighth International Joint Conference on Natural Language Processing (Volume 1: Long Papers)*, pages 733–743, Taipei, Taiwan. Asian Federation of Natural Language Processing.

Christopher D. Manning, Mihai Surdeanu, John Bauer, Jenny Finkel, Steven J. Bethard, and David McClosky. 2014. The Stanford CoreNLP natural language processing toolkit. In *Association for Computational Linguistics (ACL) System Demonstrations*, pages 55–60.

Volodymyr Mnih, Adrià Puigdomènech Badia, Mehdi Mirza, Alex Graves, Timothy P. Lillicrap, Tim Harley, David Silver, and Koray Kavukcuoglu. 2016. Asynchronous methods for deep reinforcement learning. In *International conference on machine learning*, pages 1928–1937.

Mark Neumann, Daniel King, Iz Beltagy, and Waleed Ammar. 2019. ScispaCy: Fast and robust models for biomedical natural language processing. In *Proceedings of the 18th BioNLP Workshop and Shared Task*, pages 319–327, Florence, Italy. Association for Computational Linguistics.

Enrique Noriega-Atala, Marco A. Valenzuela-Escárcega, Clayton Morrison, and Mihai Surdeanu. 2017. Learning what to read: Focused machine reading. In *Proceedings of the 2017 Conference on Empirical Methods in Natural Language Processing*, pages 2905–2910, Copenhagen, Denmark. Association for Computational Linguistics.

Lev Ratinov, Dan Roth, Doug Downey, and Mike Anderson. 2011. Local and Global Algorithms for Disambiguation to Wikipedia. In *Proc. of the Annual Meeting of the Association for Computational Linguistics (ACL)*.

Erik F. Tjong Kim Sang and Fien De Meulder. 2003. Introduction to the CoNLL-2003 shared task: Language-independent named entity recognition. In *Proceedings of the Seventh Conference on Natural Language Learning at HLT-NAACL 2003*, pages 142–147.

Haohan Wang, Xiang Liu, Yifeng Tao, Wenting Ye, Qiao Jin, William W. Cohen, and Eic P. Xing. 2019. Automatic human-like mining and constructing reliable genetic association database with deep reinforcement learning. In *PSB*, pages 112–123. World Scientific.

Johannes Welbl, Pontus Stenetorp, and Sebastian Riedel. 2018. Constructing datasets for multi-hop reading comprehension across documents. *Transactions of the Association for Computational Linguistics*, 6:287–302.

Zhilin Yang, Peng Qi, Saizheng Zhang, Yoshua Bengio, William Cohen, Ruslan Salakhutdinov, and Christopher D. Manning. 2018. HotpotQA: A dataset for diverse, explainable multi-hop question answering. In *Proceedings of the 2018 Conference on Empirical Methods in Natural Language Processing*, pages 2369–2380, Brussels, Belgium. Association for Computational Linguistics.

Table Retrieval May Not Necessitate Table-specific Model Design

Zhiruo Wang, Zhengbao Jiang, Eric Nyberg, Graham Neubig
Language Technologies Institute, Carnegie Mellon University
{zhiruow,zhengbaj,ehn,gneubig}@cs.cmu.edu

Abstract

Tables are an important form of structured data for both human and machine readers alike, providing answers to questions that cannot, or cannot easily, be found in texts. Recent work has designed special models and training paradigms for table-related tasks such as table-based question answering and table retrieval. Though effective, they add complexity in both modeling and data acquisition compared to generic text solutions and obscure which elements are truly beneficial. In this work, we focus on the task of table retrieval, and ask: "is table-specific model design necessary for table retrieval, or can a simpler text-based model be effectively used to achieve a similar result?" First, we perform an analysis on a table-based portion of the Natural Questions dataset (NQ-table), and find that structure plays a negligible role in more than 70% of the cases. Based on this, we experiment with a general Dense Passage Retriever (DPR) based on text and a specialized Dense Table Retriever (DTR) that uses table-specific model designs. We find that DPR performs well without any table-specific design and training, and even achieves superior results compared to DTR when fine-tuned on properly linearized tables. We then experiment with three modules to explicitly encode table structures, namely auxiliary row/column embeddings, hard attention masks, and soft relation-based attention biases. However, none of these yielded significant improvements, suggesting that table-specific model design may not be necessary for table retrieval.[1]

1 Introduction

Tables are a valuable form of data that organize information in a structured way for easy storage, browsing, and retrieval (Cafarella et al., 2008; Jauhar et al., 2016; Zhang and Balog, 2020). They often contain data that is organized in a more accessible manner than in unstructured texts, or even not available in text at all (Chen et al., 2020a). Therefore, tables are widely used in question answering (QA) (Pasupat and Liang, 2015; Zhong et al., 2017; Yu et al., 2018). For open-domain QA, the ability to retrieve relevant tables with target answers is crucial to the performance of end-to-end QA systems (Herzig et al., 2021). For example, in the Natural Questions (Kwiatkowski et al., 2019) dataset, 13.2% of the answerable questions can be addressed by tables and 74.4% by texts.

Question:
Who is the highest paid baseball player in the major leagues?

Table:

List of highest-paid Major League Baseball players

Name	Position	Team(s)	Salary	Ref
Clayton Kershaw	SP	Los Angeles Dodgers	$32,571,428	[15]
Justin Verlander	SP	Houston Astros	$28,000,000	[16]
Ryan Howard	1B	Philadelphia Phillies	$25,000,000	[17]
Cliff Lee	SP	Philadelphia Phillies	$25,000,000	[18]
Zack Greinke	SP	Los Angeles Dodgers	$25,000,000	[19]
Felix Hernandez	SP	Seattle Mariners	$24,907,142	[20]

Figure 1: A correct table can be identified by matching key phrases in question to those in the table title and header cells.

Because tables are intuitively different from unstructured text, most previous works consider text-based methods to be functionally incapable of processing tables effectively and create special-purpose models with table-specific architectures and training methods, adding auxiliary structure-indicative parameters (Herzig et al., 2020; Wang et al., 2021b; Deng et al., 2020; Yang et al., 2022), enforcing structure-aware attention (Yin et al., 2020; Wang et al., 2021b; Zayats et al., 2021), and table-oriented pre-training objectives (Deng et al., 2020; Yin et al., 2020; Wang et al., 2021b; Liu et al., 2021; Yu et al., 2020). Though effective in many tasks, these special-purpose models are more complex than generic solutions for textual encod-

[1]The code and data are available at https://github.com/zorazrw/nqt-retrieval

Proceedings of the Workshop on Structured and Unstructured Knowledge Integration (SUKI), pages 36 - 46
July 14, 2022

ing, and must be intentionally built for and trained on tabular data. In addition, because these methods modify both the model design and the training data, it is difficult to measure the respective contributions of each of these elements.

Particularly for question-based table retrieval, we hypothesize that content matching is paramount, and little, if any, structural understanding may be required. For example, given a question "Who is the highest paid baseball player in the major leagues?" in Figure 1, a correct table can be retrieved by simply identifying the phrase "highest-paid", "major league", and "baseball player" in the table title, and matching the semantic type of "Who" to the "Name" header. Hence, any benefit demonstrated by table-based models may well come from good training data while table-specific model design has a limited influence.

In this paper, we specifically ask: "Does table retrieval require table-specific model design, or can properly trained generic text retrievers be exploited to achieve similar performance with less added complexity?" Our work centers around the table-based open-domain QA dataset, NQ-table (Herzig et al., 2021), a subset of the Natural Questions (NQ) dataset (Kwiatkowski et al., 2019) where each question can be answered by part(s) of a Wikipedia table. We start with manual analysis of 100 random samples from NQ-table and observe that consideration of table structure seems largely unnecessary in over 70% of the cases, while the remaining 30% of cases only require simple structure understanding such as row/column alignment without structure-dependent complex reasoning chains (§ 2). With this observation, we experiment with two strong retrieval models: a general-purpose text-based retriever (DPR; Karpukhin et al. (2020)) and a special-purpose table-based retriever (DTR; Herzig et al. (2021)). We find that DPR, without any table-specific model design or training, achieves similar accuracy as the state-of-the-art table retriever DTR, and further fine-tuning on NQ-table yields significantly superior performance, casting doubt on the necessity of table-specific model design in table retrieval (§ 3). Using DPR as the base model, we then thoroughly examine the effectiveness of both encoding structure implicitly with structure-preserving table linearization (§ 4) and encoding structure explicitly with table-specific model design, such as auxiliary embeddings and specialized attention mechanisms (§ 5). We find that models can already achieve a degree of structure awareness using properly linearized tables as inputs, and additionally adding explicit structure encoding model designs does not yield a further improvement. In sum, the results reveal that a strong text-based model is competitive for table retrieval, and table-specific model designs may have limited additional benefit. This indicates the potential to directly apply future improved text retrieval systems for table retrieval, a task where they were previously considered less applicable.

2 NQ-table Analysis: How Much Structure Does Table Retrieval Require?

The NQ-table dataset (Herzig et al., 2021) is a subset of the Natural Questions (NQ) dataset (Kwiatkowski et al., 2019) which contains questions from real users that can be answered by Wikipedia articles. Previous works on text-based QA extract the text portion from source Wikipedia articles that can answer around 71k questions, while NQ-table extract tables that contain answers for 12k questions. Unless otherwise specified, we use NQ-text to denote the commonly referred NQ dataset that can be answered by texts.

To better understand to what extent (if any) is structure understanding required by table retrieval, we perform a manual analysis on the NQ-table dataset. Specifically, we randomly sample 100 questions and their relevant tables then categorize their matching patterns.

Keyword Matching Without Structural Concern Aligning with the insight that retrieval often emphasizes content matching rather than complex reasoning (Rogers et al., 2021), we find that 71 out of the 100 samples only require simple keyword matching, where 18 questions fully match with table titles (Figure 2 (a)) and the other 53 questions further match with table headers (Figure 2 (b)).

Retrieval that Requires Row/Column Alignment For the other 29 samples, understanding table structure is helpful but only simple row/column alignment is needed. 21 of them require locating content cells in a specific column and combining the information from headers. For example in Figure 2(c), under the general header "Population", one should locate the "Total" field by their structural relation to confirm that the 'total number' measure of 'population' exists. In addition, 7 of the samples are some-

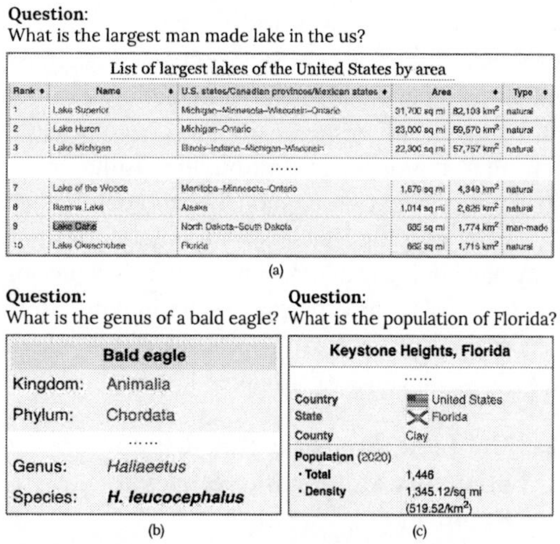

Figure 2: Table (a) matches the question by its title, (b) matches topic in title and answer type in header, and in (c) knowing the column alignment helps.

what ambiguous and may require external knowledge or question clarification (Min et al., 2020).

In summary, our analysis reveals that understanding table structure is not necessary in the majority of cases, and even for cases where structural information is useful, they merely require aligning the rows/columns instead of building complex chains of reasoning.

3 Text Retrieval vs Table Retrieval

Given the previous analysis, we hypothesize that general-purpose text-based retrievers without table-specific designs might not be necessarily worse than special-purpose table-based retrievers, contradictory to what most previous work has assumed (Herzig et al., 2021, 2020; Yin et al., 2020; Wang et al., 2021b). Properly trained text-based retrievers might even outperform table-based retrievers because the strong content matching ability learned on text retrieval datasets can transfer to the table retrieval task.

To validate these assumptions, we examine two representative retrieval systems: the text-based Dense Passage Retriever (DPR) and the table-based Dense Table Retriever (DTR). We first briefly introduce their input formats and model architectures (§ 3.1,§ 3.2), then conduct experiments in both zero-shot and fine-tuning settings and compare their table retrieval performance (§ 3.3).

3.1 Text Retriever: DPR

We choose DPR (Karpukhin et al., 2020) as a representative text retrieval model, mainly because of (1) its impressive performance across many text-related retrieval tasks, and (2) its similarity with DTR from both training and modeling perspectives, which make it easy to make fair comparisons.

DPR comprises a question-context bi-encoder built on BERT (Devlin et al., 2018), which includes three types of input embeddings as summarized in Table 1. The question encoder BERT_q encodes each question $\boldsymbol{q}$ and outputs its dense representation using the representation of [CLS] token, denoted as $\boldsymbol{h_q} = \text{BERT}_q(\boldsymbol{q})[\text{CLS}]$. The context encoder works similarly. To enable tables for sequential context inputs, we linearize each table into a token sequence $\boldsymbol{T}$, which is then fed into the context encoder BERT_c to obtain its dense representation $\boldsymbol{h_T} = \text{BERT}_c(T)[\text{CLS}]$. The similarity score between a question $\boldsymbol{q}$ and a table $\boldsymbol{T}$ is computed as the dot product of two vectors $sim(\boldsymbol{q}, T) = \boldsymbol{h_q} \cdot \boldsymbol{h_T}$.

DPR has been trained only on sequential text contexts. For each question in the NQ-text training set, the model is trained to select the correct context that contains the answer from a curated batch of contexts including both the annotated correct contexts and mined hard negative contexts.

To convert tables into the DPR input format, we linearize tables into token sequences. We concatenate the title, the header row, and subsequent content rows using a period '.' (row delimiter). Within each header or content row, we concatenate adjacent cell strings using a vertical bar '|' (cell delimiter). A template table linearization reads as $[\text{title}].[\text{header}].[\text{content}_1]. \cdots .[\text{content}_n]$. Although the BERT encoder has the capacity for a maximum of 512 tokens, DPR is only exposed to contexts no longer than 100 words during training and testing. To avoid potential discrepancies between its original training and our inference procedure, we shorten long tables by selecting the first few rows that fit into the 100-word window.

3.2 Table Retriever: DTR

Dense Table Retriever (DTR) (Herzig et al., 2021) is the current state-of-the-art table retrieval model on the NQ-table dataset.

Model Architecture DTR largely follows the bi-encoder structure of DPR, but differs from it in the embedding layer. As shown in Table 1, DTR utilizes the existing embeddings in alternative ways and introduces new types of embeddings specifically designed to encode tables.

Both models use the BERT vocabulary index for token embedding. For the segment index, DPR assigns all tokens in a sequence to index 0, while DTR distinguishes the title from table content by assigning 0 and 1, respectively. For positions, DPR inherits from BERT the sequence-wise order index $[0, 1, 2, ..., \text{sequence length}-1]$; DTR adopts a cell-wise reset strategy that records the index of a token within its located cell $[0, 1, ..., \text{cell length} - 1]$.

Most importantly, DTR introduces row and column embeddings to encode the structural position of each token in the cell that it appears. This explicit join of three positional embeddings is potentially more powerful than the BERT-style flat index. Besides, concerning the high frequency of numerical values in tables, DTR adds a ranking index for each token if it is part of a number.

Embeddings	DPR	DTR
token	BERT vocab	BERT vocab
segment	0 for all tokens	0 for text, 1 for table
position	sequential	cell-wise reset
row	-	row index
column	-	column index
rank	-	rank of token value

Table 1: Comparison of DPR and DTR embeddings.

Training Process DTR also has a more complex training process than DPR. As summarized in Figure 3, DTR has a three-stage training using tables.

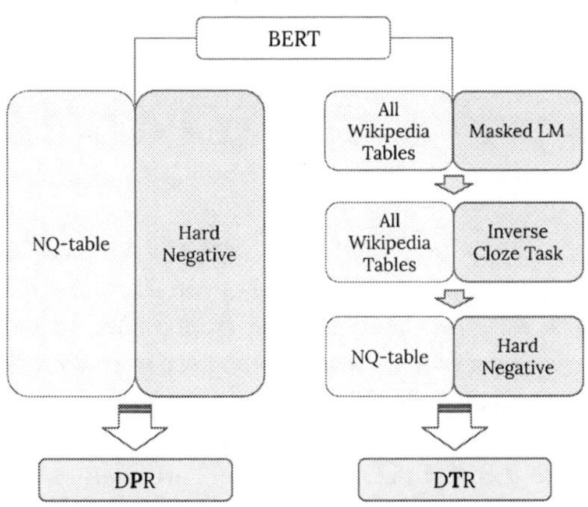

Figure 3: Comparison of DPR and DTR training.

First, model parameters, except for those extra table-specific embeddings, are initialized with BERT weights. The model is then pre-trained on all Wikipedia tables using the Masked LM (MLM) (Devlin et al., 2018) task, yielding the TAPAS (Herzig et al., 2020) model. Second, to leverage TAPAS to the retrieval task, it is further pre-trained using the Inverse Cloze task (ICT) introduced by ORQA (Lee et al., 2019), again, on all Wikipedia tables. Third, the model is trained on the specific NQ-table dataset, similar to the way that DPR is trained on text retrieval datasets: for each question in the NQ-table training set, DTR uses the annotated table as the positive context and self-mined tables without answers as hard negative (HN) contexts.

3.3 Text Retrieval Benefits Table Retrieval

To evaluate the benefit on table retrieval from training on in-domain text retrieval datasets, we compare the performance of DPR and BERT (Devlin et al., 2018) after fine-tuning on NQ-table.

As shown in Table 3, *BERT-table* significantly underperforms *DPR-table*, indicating that training on in-domain text retrieval datasets benefits the table retrieval task. We conjecture that the large gap is essentially because (1) NQ-text and NQ-table questions share similar characteristics hence are agnostic to the format of answer source (Wolfson et al., 2020), and (2) NQ-text has a larger size than NQ-table (71k versus 12k).

3.4 DPR vs DTR

To verify if table-specific model designs in DTR are necessary, we start with comparing the original DPR with DTR to evaluate their off-the-shelf performance, then proceed to fine-tune DPR on NQ-table to examine the how much improvement can be brought by training data. We evaluate both models on NQ-table test set and measure the retrieval accuracy by computing the portion of questions where the top-k retrieved tables contain the answer.

For DPR experiments, we use the latest published checkpoint[2] where the hard-negative text passages are mined using the DPR checkpoint saved in the previous round. To reproduce the DTR performance, we use the published checkpoints[3] and run the retrieval inference.

To curate training samples for questions in the NQ-table training set, we take the same positive table used in DTR training. For negative contexts,

[2]https://github.com/facebookresearch/DPR

[3]https://github.com/google-research/tapas/blob/master/DENSE_TABLE_RETRIEVER.md

we use the original DPR checkpoint to retrieve the top-100 table candidates for each question, from which we take the highest-ranked tables without answers as the hard negatives. We train with a batch size of 16 and a learning rate of 2e−5. Experiments are finished on four NVIDIA Tesla V100 GPUs.

Note that the published DPR and DTR checkpoints are not strictly comparable, since the size of DPR base falls between the DTR medium and DTR large with respect to the number of parameters. We report the performance of DTR in both medium and large size to approximate the lower and upper bounds for the DTR base model.

Size	Layers	Attention Heads	Hidden Size
medium	8	8	512
base	12	8	768
large	24	16	1024

Table 2: Hyper-parameters for BERT models of varied sizes. Models of different sizes vary in the number of transformer layers, the number of heads in the self-attention module, and the dimension of hidden states.

Table 2 shows the configurations of BERT-variants in different sizes. As can be seen from the hyper-parameter values, models of medium size have the smallest capacity, base is an intermediate configuration, and large size is the biggest.

As reported in Table 3, DPR is able to achieve a zero-shot retrieval accuracy (*DPR*) on NQ-table that is fairly close to the state-of-the-art DTR model, even without any table-specific model design and training. Further, simply fine-tuning DPR on NQ-table (*DPR-table*) using the same annotated positive and mined hard-negative tables as DTR increases the performance by a large margin, achieving superior performance than DTR, especially at top ranking positions (i.e., small k).

Model	Retrieval Accuracy				
	@1	@5	@10	@20	@50
DTR (medium)	62.32	82.51	86.75	91.51	94.26
DTR (large)	63.98	84.27	**89.65**	**93.48**	**95.65**
BERT-table	60.97	79.81	85.51	88.20	91.62
DPR	57.04	80.54	86.13	89.54	92.34
DPR-table	**67.91**	**84.89**	88.72	90.58	92.86

Table 3: Top-k table retrieval accuracy on NQ-table test set. *DPR* is the original model checkpoint. *DPR-table* and *BERT-table* are DPR and BERT fine-tuned on NQ-table respectively.

These observations question the necessity of both table-specific model designs listed in Table 1 and table-specific pre-training listed in Figure 3. Given the task analysis in § 2 that table retrieval only requires simple structure understanding, we hypothesize that DPR, trained with table inputs linearized from top-to-bottom and left-to-right, is functionally capable of implicitly encoding simple table structure such as row/column alignment, and the benefit of extra table-specific model designs is minimal. To thoroughly and rigorously verify our hypothesis, we first examine the effect of different ordering in table linearization in § 4, then experiment with three widely-used structure injection model designs by adding them on DPR in § 5.

4 Implicit Structure Encoding from Linearized Tables

The simplest way to encode table structure is to linearize the table following the top-to-bottom left-to-right order and insert delimiters between cells and rows, from which the sequence-oriented transformer models should also be able to recover the two-dimensional table structure.

We hypothesize that this type of implicit structure encoding is sufficient for table retrieval, which only requires simple structure understanding. To verify this, we manipulate linearized tables by randomly shuffling their rows/columns (§ 4.1) or removing the delimiters (§ 4.2), and examine how these perturbation affect the final performance.

4.1 Shuffling Rows and Columns

Our first experiment focuses on the order of table linearization: if DPR relies on a proper linearization to capture table structure, randomly shuffling the table contents should corrupt the structure information and hurt the representation quality, leading to lower retrieval accuracy.

To verify this, we shuffle table cells within each *row*, each *column*, or *both*. Cells in the same row often describe the same entity from multiple properties according to their column headers, therefore shuffling the order of multiple cells in the same row corrupts their alignment with header cells. Meanwhile, cells in the same column are often of the same semantic type but are attributes to different entities in different rows, shuffling the order of cells in the same column breaks their alignment with entities. We also examine shuffling on both dimensions, which completely removes the order information from the table linearizations.

Since models trained on properly linearized tables might be prone to the train-test discrepancy when tested on shuffled tables, we conjecture that the gap between testing on proper tables and shuffled tables cannot be fully attributed to the loss of order information. We therefore conduct a more rigorous experiment by fine-tuning DPR on shuffled tables in both dimensions (*DPR-table w/ shuffle*) and test it on both proper and shuffled tables.

Method		Retrieval Accuracy				
Model	**Shuffle**	**@1**	**@5**	**@10**	**@20**	**@50**
DPR	-	57.04	80.54	86.13	89.54	92.34
	row	55.18	79.19	85.82	89.75	92.44
	column	57.04	80.85	86.65	89.34	92.55
	both	57.97	79.61	84.89	89.44	92.55
DPR-table	-	67.91	84.89	88.72	90.58	92.86
	row	55.18	76.09	80.64	85.40	89.23
	column	58.39	77.74	82.92	86.44	89.86
	both	54.76	75.16	80.64	84.87	88.82
DPR-table w/ shuffle	-	62.94	80.12	84.99	88.92	91.30
	row	62.11	80.95	85.30	88.82	91.72
	column	64.91	82.30	86.75	89.54	92.55
	both	63.35	81.06	85.20	89.34	91.93

Table 4: Top-k table retrieval accuracy on shuffled NQ tables, using the original *DPR*, the fine-tuned (*DPR-table*), and the fine-tuned on shuffled tables (*DPR-table w/ shuffle*).

As shown in Table 4, on the original DPR model, all table shuffling strategies result in minor variations in retrieval accuracy, which is intuitive because DPR has never been trained on linearized tables and it is not sensitive to cell orders.

The performance of fine-tuned DPR (*DPR-table*) drops significantly when tested on shuffled tables, similar to the previous finding that T5 model is also sensitive to the ordering of structured knowledge (Xie et al., 2022). Besides the potential discrepancy in table layout between training and test inputs, this may indicate that DPR, although without explicit structure encoding modules, also learns to implicitly capture structures by training on linearized table inputs.

To ablate out the influence of train-test discrepancy, we also fine-tune DPR on shuffled positive and negative tables. As expected, *DPR-table w/ shuffle* does not suffer from train-test discrepancy. While DPR fine-tuned on shuffled tables still outperforms the original DPR (57.04→62.94@1), the improvement is not as significant as the improvement obtained by fine-tuning on proper tables (57.04→67.91@1), indicating that DPR is able to utilize structure-preserving table linearizations to encode structures during training.

Comparing different shuffling dimensions, we notice that in-*row* shuffling hurts the performance more than in-*column* shuffling, indicating that preserving semantic type alignment within each column is more important than preserving entity alignment within each row for table retrieval.

4.2 Removing Delimiters Between Rows/Cells

In this section, we study the impact of delimiters in helping models to encode table structures. If delimiters are not included, it is theoretically impossible to recover the table structure even from properly linearized tables, because the boundaries between different cells and rows are unknown. To verify if delimiters can serve as effective indicators of table structure, we study the usefulness of both inserting delimiter ('|') between cells and inserting delimiter ('.') between rows.

Similarly to the previous experiment, we evaluate (1) the original DPR model (*DPR*), (2) the DPR fine-tuned on tables with delimiters (*DPR-table*), and (3) the one fine-tuned on linearized tables without delimiters (*DPR-table w/o delimiter*).

Method		Retrieval Accuracy				
Model	**Delimiter**	**@1**	**@5**	**@10**	**@20**	**@50**
DPR	all	57.04	80.54	86.13	89.54	92.34
	cell	56.00	79.40	85.30	89.54	92.34
	row	54.24	77.54	82.92	87.68	92.13
	none	55.49	79.09	84.78	89.44	92.03
DPR-table	all	67.91	84.89	88.72	90.58	92.86
	cell	55.80	75.26	81.16	85.20	89.23
	row	55.07	74.95	80.75	84.68	89.65
	none	56.63	76.19	81.26	86.13	89.75
DPR-table w/o delimiter	all	63.46	81.47	85.09	88.82	92.13
	cell	63.04	83.02	87.47	90.06	92.13
	row	63.35	80.54	85.20	89.34	92.03
	none	64.49	81.88	86.23	89.86	92.55

Table 5: NQ-table retrieval accuracy with linearized table w/ and w/o cell and row delimiters. *cell* linearizes table by only inserting delimiters between cells, *row* only inserts delimiters between rows, and *none* inserts neither.

As shown in Table 5, for *DPR*, although the overall performance drop is small without delimiters, separating cells is more important than separating rows, which is intuitive because the number of cells is larger than the number of rows. On *DPR-table* that learns from properly delimited tables, the influence is more significant, and the extent of dropping is similar to that of table structure shuffling in Table 4. Also similar to the previous findings, training on non-delimited tables (*DPR-table w/o delimiter*) improves over the original DPR, but the improvement is not as significant as the improvement obtained by fine-tuning on delimited tables, suggesting that cell and row delimiters help models encode table structure.

5 Explicit Structure Encoding with Table-specific Model Design

From the previous section, we conclude that DPR can already encode simple table structures based on structure-preserving linearized tables with correct cell order and delimiters. The next question is "can explicit table-specific model designs encode more complex structure that is useful beyond the capacity of implicit encoding?"

In this section, we examine three widely used table-specific modules to explicitly encode table structure information by adding these modules on top of the DPR architecture. As summarized in Table 6 and illustrated in Figure 4, we categorize existing methods for table-specific structure encoding into three representative types: (1) auxiliary table-specific embeddings, (2) restricted hard attention mask to enforce structure-aware attention, and (3) soft attention bias based on the structural relations of cell pairs. For each component, we add it onto the DPR architecture and fine-tune under the same setting as for *DPR-table*.

Method	Papers
auxiliary embeddings	TAPAS (Herzig et al., 2020) MATE (Eisenschlos et al., 2021) TUTA (Wang et al., 2021b) TABBIE (Iida et al., 2021)
hard attention mask	TURL (Deng et al., 2020) SAT (Zhang et al., 2020) ETC (Ainslie et al., 2020) DoT (Krichene et al., 2021) MATE (Eisenschlos et al., 2021) TUTA (Wang et al., 2021b)
soft attention bias	RAT-SQL (Wang et al., 2020) TableFormer (Yang et al., 2022)

Table 6: Structure encoding methods used in previous works for table-related tasks.

5.1 Auxiliary Row and Columns Embeddings

We first examine if adding table-specific embedding parameters would bring additional improvement. Specifically, we add row and column embeddings into the DPR to encode the row and column indices of tokens, which is denoted as *DPR-table w/ emb*. Both row and column indices are 1-indexed, and 0 is used for tokens that are not part of the table (e.g., title). We initialize row/column embeddings with zero to allow smooth continual learning.

5.2 Hard Attention Mask

Another approach is to enforce structure-aware attention using hard attention mask that only allows attention between elements within their mutual structural proximity, with the assumption that elements are only semantically relevant to elements in their structural proximity. Specifically, Krichene et al. (2021); Eisenschlos et al. (2021); Deng et al. (2020) sparsify the attention mask such that each token is only visible to other tokens that are either within the same row or the same column. We apply this masking strategy when fine-tuning DPR and denote this setting as *DPR-table w/ mask*.

5.3 Soft Relation-based Attention Bias

The third method is to bias the attention weight between two tokens based on their structural relation, which is a more fine-grained way to enforce structure-aware attention than hard mask. Specifically, different bias scalars are added to the attention scores based on the relation between two cells. Wang et al. (2020) categorize relations by columns, while Yang et al. (2022) defines 13 relations based on which component the token belongs to: sentence, header, and cell. A more concrete example is illustrated in Figure 4. Relational bias is invariant to the numerical indices of rows and columns, which is more robust to answer-invariant structure perturbation. We follow Yang et al. (2022) to add soft attention bias on DPR with 13 relations.

5.4 Results and Analysis

As shown in Table 7, methods that explicitly encode table structures, either with additional row/column embeddings (*w/ emb*), hard attention mask (*w/ mask*), or soft relation-based attention bias (*w/ bias*), do not bring improvements over the *DPR-table* baseline, indicating that given the capacity of DPR in implicitly encoding structure

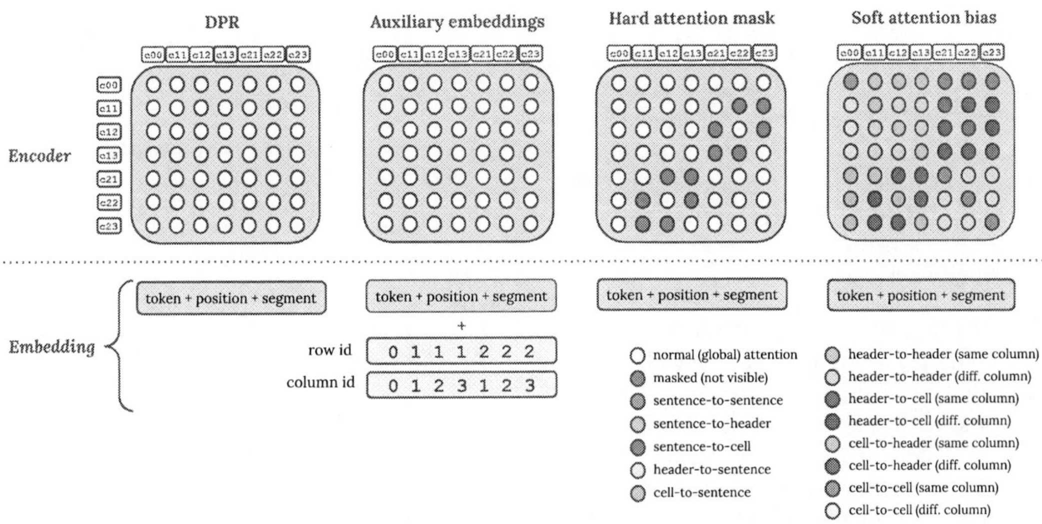

Figure 4: Illustration of three explicit structure encoding methods.

from linearized tables, the benefit of using special-purpose structure encoding modules is minimal.

Model	Retrieval Accuracy @1	@5	@10	@20	@50
DPR-table	**67.91**	**84.89**	**88.72**	**90.58**	92.86
w/ emb	65.73	81.99	86.02	89.23	92.86
w/ mask	62.11	81.88	86.96	89.86	**93.06**
w/ bias	65.42	82.23	86.75	89.54	92.13

Table 7: Top-k table retrieval accuracy on NQ-table test. *DPR-table* is fine-tuned on the NQ-table without any table-specific modules, while the other three methods add auxiliary row/column embeddings (*w/ emb*), hard attention mask (*w/ mask*), and soft relation-based attention bias respectively (*w/ bias*).

6 Related Work

Open-domain Question Answering Open-domain QA systems often use a retriever-reader pipeline, where the retriever retrieves relevant contexts and the reader extracts or generates answer from them. Because the candidate context corpus is usually large with millions of documents, good retrieval accuracy is crucial for open-domain QA systems (Karpukhin et al., 2020). Beyond texts, another common sources for answering open-domain questions is tables. Herzig et al. (2021) recently identified a subset of Natural Questions (NQ) dataset (Kwiatkowski et al., 2019) that is answerable by Wikipedia tables. Oguz et al. (2021) found that incorporating structured knowledge is beneficial for open-domain QA tasks. Ma et al. (2021) showed that verbalizing structured knowledge into fluent text bring further gains over raw format for open-domain QA. Different from prior work, our paper analyzes different strategies for encoding tables with a focus on the task of table retrieval.

Table Understanding To encode the relational structure of tables, CNNs (Chen et al., 2019a), RNNs (Gol et al., 2019), LSTMs (Fetahu et al., 2019), and their combinations (Chen et al., 2019b) are explored. In addition, graph neural networks (GNN) are used, especially for tables with complex structures (Koci et al., 2018; Zayats et al., 2021; Vu et al., 2021; Bhagavatula et al., 2015). With the recent advances in pre-trained language models, table encoders adapt pre-trained language models with additional table-specific modules encoding structure (Herzig et al., 2020; Yin et al., 2020; Wang et al., 2021b) and numeracy (Wang et al., 2021b; Herzig et al., 2020). These methods are intentionally built for tables, but their necessity in each task remains unknown. Our work exploits a generic model to show that content-emphasized tasks like retrieval do not require such specific designs.

Table Retrieval Earlier works focus on web table search in response to keyword queries (Cafarella et al., 2008, 2009; Balakrishnan et al., 2015; Pimplikar and Sarawagi, 2012) or a seed table (Sarmad et al., 2012). Many of them use the 60 keywords and relevant web tables collected by Zhang and Balog (2018). Tables are modeled by aggregating multiple fields (Zhang et al., 2019), contexts (Trabelsi et al., 2019), and synthesized schema labels (Chen et al., 2020b). More recently, Chen et al. (2020c); Wang et al. (2021a) use structure-augmented BERT for retrieval. These works largely treat the retrieval task on its own account and target similarity under the traditional Information Retrieval (IR).

7 Conclusion

Given the importance of finding relevant tables when answering questions in the NQ-table dataset, we study the task of table retrieval and find that table retrieval emphasizes content rather than table structure. Our experiments with the text-generic Dense Passage Retriever (DPR) and the state-of-the-art table-specific Dense Table Retriever (DTR) demonstrate that DPR can already encode simple structures based on linearized tables and table-specific designs such as auxiliary embeddings, hard attention mask, and soft attention bias are not necessary. Our findings suggest that future development on table retrieval can potentially be built upon successful text retrievers and table-specific model designs should be carefully examined to avoid unnecessary complexity.

Acknowledgements

We would like to thank Frank F. Xu and Kaixin Ma for the helpful discussions and anonymous reviewers for their valuable suggestions on this paper.

References

Joshua Ainslie, Santiago Ontanon, Chris Alberti, Vaclav Cvicek, Zachary Fisher, Philip Pham, Anirudh Ravula, Sumit Sanghai, Qifan Wang, and Li Yang. 2020. Etc: Encoding long and structured inputs in transformers. In *Proceedings of the 2020 Conference on Empirical Methods in Natural Language Processing (EMNLP)*, pages 268–284.

Sreeram Balakrishnan, Alon Halevy, Boulos Harb, Hongrae Lee, Jayant Madhavan, Afshin Rostamizadeh, Warren Shen, Kenneth Wilder, Fei Wu, and Cong Yu. 2015. Applying webtables in practice.

Chandra Sekhar Bhagavatula, Thanapon Noraset, and Doug Downey. 2015. Tabel: Entity linking in web tables. In *International Semantic Web Conference*, pages 425–441. Springer.

Michael J Cafarella, Alon Halevy, and Nodira Khoussainova. 2009. Data integration for the relational web. *Proceedings of the VLDB Endowment*, 2(1):1090–1101.

Michael J Cafarella, Alon Halevy, Daisy Zhe Wang, Eugene Wu, and Yang Zhang. 2008. Webtables: exploring the power of tables on the web. *Proceedings of the VLDB Endowment*, 1(1):538–549.

Jiaoyan Chen, Ernesto Jiménez-Ruiz, Ian Horrocks, and Charles Sutton. 2019a. Colnet: Embedding the semantics of web tables for column type prediction. In *Proceedings of the AAAI Conference on Artificial Intelligence*, volume 33, pages 29–36.

Jiaoyan Chen, Ernesto Jiménez-Ruiz, Ian Horrocks, and Charles Sutton. 2019b. Learning semantic annotations for tabular data. *arXiv preprint arXiv:1906.00781*.

Wenhu Chen, Hanwen Zha, Zhiyu Chen, Wenhan Xiong, Hong Wang, and William Wang. 2020a. Hybridqa: A dataset of multi-hop question answering over tabular and textual data. *arXiv preprint arXiv:2004.07347*.

Zhiyu Chen, Haiyan Jia, Jeff Heflin, and Brian D Davison. 2020b. Leveraging schema labels to enhance dataset search. *Advances in Information Retrieval*, 12035:267.

Zhiyu Chen, Mohamed Trabelsi, Jeff Heflin, Yinan Xu, and Brian D Davison. 2020c. Table search using a deep contextualized language model. In *Proceedings of the 43rd International ACM SIGIR Conference on Research and Development in Information Retrieval*, pages 589–598.

Xiang Deng, Huan Sun, Alyssa Lees, You Wu, and Cong Yu. 2020. Turl: Table understanding through representation learning. *arXiv preprint arXiv:2006.14806*.

Jacob Devlin, Ming-Wei Chang, Kenton Lee, and Kristina Toutanova. 2018. Bert: Pre-training of deep bidirectional transformers for language understanding. *arXiv preprint arXiv:1810.04805*.

Julian Eisenschlos, Maharshi Gor, Thomas Mueller, and William Cohen. 2021. Mate: Multi-view attention for table transformer efficiency. In *Proceedings of the 2021 Conference on Empirical Methods in Natural Language Processing*, pages 7606–7619.

Besnik Fetahu, Avishek Anand, and Maria Koutraki. 2019. Tablenet: An approach for determining fine-grained relations for wikipedia tables. In *The World Wide Web Conference*, pages 2736–2742.

Majid Ghasemi Gol, Jay Pujara, and Pedro Szekely. 2019. Tabular cell classification using pre-trained cell embeddings. In *2019 IEEE International Conference on Data Mining (ICDM)*, pages 230–239. IEEE.

Jonathan Herzig, Thomas Müller, Syrine Krichene, and Julian Martin Eisenschlos. 2021. Open domain question answering over tables via dense retrieval. *arXiv preprint arXiv:2103.12011*.

Jonathan Herzig, Pawel Krzysztof Nowak, Thomas Mueller, Francesco Piccinno, and Julian Eisenschlos. 2020. Tapas: Weakly supervised table parsing via pre-training. In *Proceedings of the 58th Annual Meeting of the Association for Computational Linguistics*, pages 4320–4333.

Hiroshi Iida, Dung Thai, Varun Manjunatha, and Mohit Iyyer. 2021. Tabbie: Pretrained representations of tabular data. In *Proceedings of the 2021 Conference of the North American Chapter of the Association for Computational Linguistics: Human Language Technologies*, pages 3446–3456.

Sujay Kumar Jauhar, Peter Turney, and Eduard Hovy. 2016. Tables as semi-structured knowledge for question answering. In *Proceedings of the 54th Annual Meeting of the Association for Computational Linguistics (Volume 1: Long Papers)*, pages 474–483.

Vladimir Karpukhin, Barlas Oguz, Sewon Min, Patrick Lewis, Ledell Wu, Sergey Edunov, Danqi Chen, and Wen-tau Yih. 2020. Dense passage retrieval for open-domain question answering. In *Proceedings of the 2020 Conference on Empirical Methods in Natural Language Processing (EMNLP)*, pages 6769–6781.

Elvis Koci, Maik Thiele, Wolfgang Lehner, and Oscar Romero. 2018. Table recognition in spreadsheets via a graph representation. In *2018 13th IAPR International Workshop on Document Analysis Systems (DAS)*, pages 139–144. IEEE.

Syrine Krichene, Thomas Mueller, and Julian Eisenschlos. 2021. Dot: An efficient double transformer for nlp tasks with tables. In *Findings of the Association for Computational Linguistics: ACL-IJCNLP 2021*, pages 3273–3283.

Tom Kwiatkowski, Jennimaria Palomaki, Olivia Redfield, Michael Collins, Ankur Parikh, Chris Alberti, Danielle Epstein, Illia Polosukhin, Jacob Devlin, Kenton Lee, et al. 2019. Natural questions: a benchmark for question answering research. *Transactions of the Association for Computational Linguistics*, 7:453–466.

Kenton Lee, Ming-Wei Chang, and Kristina Toutanova. 2019. Latent retrieval for weakly supervised open domain question answering. In *Proceedings of the 57th Annual Meeting of the Association for Computational Linguistics*, pages 6086–6096.

Qian Liu, Bei Chen, Jiaqi Guo, Zeqi Lin, and Jianguang Lou. 2021. Tapex: Table pre-training via learning a neural sql executor. *arXiv preprint arXiv:2107.07653*.

Kaixin Ma, Hao Cheng, Xiaodong Liu, Eric Nyberg, and Jianfeng Gao. 2021. Open domain question answering with a unified knowledge interface. *arXiv preprint arXiv:2110.08417*.

Sewon Min, Julian Michael, Hannaneh Hajishirzi, and Luke Zettlemoyer. 2020. Ambigqa: Answering ambiguous open-domain questions. In *Proceedings of the 2020 Conference on Empirical Methods in Natural Language Processing (EMNLP)*, pages 5783–5797.

Barlas Oguz, Xilun Chen, Vladimir Karpukhin, Stan Peshterliev, Dmytro Okhonko, Michael Schlichtkrull, Sonal Gupta, Yashar Mehdad, and Scott Yih. 2021. Unik-qa: Unified representations of structured and unstructured knowledge for open-domain question answering. *arXiv preprint arXiv:2012.14610*, 54:57–60.

Panupong Pasupat and Percy Liang. 2015. Compositional semantic parsing on semi-structured tables. In *Proceedings of the 53rd Annual Meeting of the Association for Computational Linguistics and the 7th International Joint Conference on Natural Language Processing (Volume 1: Long Papers)*, pages 1470–1480.

Rakesh Pimplikar and Sunita Sarawagi. 2012. Answering table queries on the web using column keywords. *Proceedings of the VLDB Endowment*, 5(10):908–919.

Anna Rogers, Matt Gardner, and Isabelle Augenstein. 2021. Qa dataset explosion: A taxonomy of nlp resources for question answering and reading comprehension. *arXiv preprint arXiv:2107.12708*.

Anish Das Sarmad, Lujun Fang, Nitin Guptad, Alon Halevyd, Hongrae Leed, Fei Wud, Reynold Xin, and Cong Yud. 2012. Finding related tables.

Mohamed Trabelsi, Brian D Davison, and Jeff Heflin. 2019. Improved table retrieval using multiple context embeddings for attributes. In *2019 IEEE International Conference on Big Data (Big Data)*, pages 1238–1244. IEEE.

Binh Vu, Craig A Knoblock, Pedro Szekely, Minh Pham, and Jay Pujara. 2021. A graph-based approach for inferring semantic descriptions of wikipedia tables. In *International Semantic Web Conference*, pages 304–320. Springer.

Bailin Wang, Richard Shin, Xiaodong Liu, Oleksandr Polozov, and Matthew Richardson. 2020. Rat-sql: Relation-aware schema encoding and linking for text-to-sql parsers. In *Proceedings of the 58th Annual Meeting of the Association for Computational Linguistics*, pages 7567–7578.

Fei Wang, Kexuan Sun, Muhao Chen, Jay Pujara, and Pedro Szekely. 2021a. Retrieving complex tables with multi-granular graph representation learning. *arXiv preprint arXiv:2105.01736*.

Zhiruo Wang, Haoyu Dong, Ran Jia, Jia Li, Zhiyi Fu, Shi Han, and Dongmei Zhang. 2021b. Tuta: Tree-based transformers for generally structured table pre-training. In *Proceedings of the 27th ACM SIGKDD Conference on Knowledge Discovery & Data Mining*, pages 1780–1790.

Tomer Wolfson, Mor Geva, Ankit Gupta, Matt Gardner, Yoav Goldberg, Daniel Deutch, and Jonathan Berant. 2020. Break it down: A question understanding benchmark. *Transactions of the Association for Computational Linguistics*, 8:183–198.

Tianbao Xie, Chen Henry Wu, Peng Shi, Ruiqi Zhong, Torsten Scholak, Michihiro Yasunaga, Chien-Sheng Wu, Ming Zhong, Pengcheng Yin, Sida I Wang, et al. 2022. Unifiedskg: Unifying and multi-tasking structured knowledge grounding with text-to-text language models. *arXiv preprint arXiv:2201.05966*.

Jingfeng Yang, Aditya Gupta, Shyam Upadhyay, Luheng He, Rahul Goel, and Shachi Paul. 2022. Tableformer: Robust transformer modeling for table-text encoding. *arXiv preprint arXiv:2203.00274*.

Pengcheng Yin, Graham Neubig, Wen-tau Yih, and Sebastian Riedel. 2020. Tabert: Pretraining for joint understanding of textual and tabular data. In *Proceedings of the 58th Annual Meeting of the Association for Computational Linguistics*, pages 8413–8426.

Tao Yu, Chien-Sheng Wu, Xi Victoria Lin, Yi Chern Tan, Xinyi Yang, Dragomir Radev, Caiming Xiong, et al. 2020. Grappa: Grammar-augmented pre-training for table semantic parsing. In *International Conference on Learning Representations*.

Tao Yu, Rui Zhang, Kai Yang, Michihiro Yasunaga, Dongxu Wang, Zifan Li, James Ma, Irene Li, Qingning Yao, Shanelle Roman, et al. 2018. Spider: A large-scale human-labeled dataset for complex and cross-domain semantic parsing and text-to-sql task. In *Proceedings of the 2018 Conference on Empirical Methods in Natural Language Processing*, pages 3911–3921.

Vicky Zayats, Kristina Toutanova, and Mari Ostendorf. 2021. Representations for question answering from documents with tables and text. *arXiv preprint arXiv:2101.10573*.

Hongzhi Zhang, Yingyao Wang, Sirui Wang, Xuezhi Cao, Fuzheng Zhang, and Zhongyuan Wang. 2020. Table fact verification with structure-aware transformer. In *Proceedings of the 2020 Conference on Empirical Methods in Natural Language Processing (EMNLP)*, pages 1624–1629.

Li Zhang, Shuo Zhang, and Krisztian Balog. 2019. Table2vec: Neural word and entity embeddings for table population and retrieval. In *Proceedings of the 42nd International ACM SIGIR Conference on Research and Development in Information Retrieval*, pages 1029–1032.

Shuo Zhang and Krisztian Balog. 2018. Ad hoc table retrieval using semantic similarity. In *Proceedings of the 2018 world wide web conference*, pages 1553–1562.

Shuo Zhang and Krisztian Balog. 2020. Web table extraction, retrieval, and augmentation: A survey. *ACM Transactions on Intelligent Systems and Technology (TIST)*, 11(2):1–35.

Victor Zhong, Caiming Xiong, and Richard Socher. 2017. Seq2sql: Generating structured queries from natural language using reinforcement learning. *arXiv preprint arXiv:1709.00103*.

Transfer Learning and Masked Generation for Answer Verbalization

Sebastien Montella
Orange Innovation / Lannion, France
Aix-Marseille Univ. CNRS, LIS / Marseille, France
sebastien.montella@orange.com

Lina M. Rojas-Barahona
Orange Innovation / Lannion, France
linamaria.rojasbarahona@orange.com

Frederic Bechet
AMU/CNRS/LIS, Marseille, France
frederic.bechet@lis-lab.fr

Johannes Heinecke
Orange Innovation / Lannion, France
johannes.heinecke@orange.com

Alexis Nasr
AMU/CNRS/LIS, Marseille, France
alexis.nasr@lis-lab.fr

Abstract

Structured Knowledge has recently emerged as an essential component to support fine-grained Question Answering (QA). In general, QA systems query a Knowledge Base (KB) to detect and extract the raw answers as final prediction. However, as lacking of context, language generation can offer a much informative and complete response. In this paper, we propose to combine the power of transfer learning and the advantage of entity placeholders to produce high-quality verbalization of extracted answers from a structured KB. We claim that such approach is especially well-suited for answer generation. Our experiments show 44.25%, 3.26% and 29.10% relative gain in BLEU over the state-of-the-art on the VQuAnDA, ParaQA and VANiLLa datasets, respectively. We additionally provide minor hallucinations corrections in VANiLLa standing for 5% of each of the training and testing set. We witness a median absolute gain of 0.81 SacreBLEU. This strengthens the importance of data quality when using automated evaluation.

1 Introduction

Question Answering (QA) has witnessed a massive number of stupendous improvements over the past few years which marked a new era of QA. At the core of this significant progress is the huge leap in the use of Pretrained Language Model (PLM). On several benchmarks, state-of-the art QA systems perform on par with human according to reported evaluation metrics. However, despite remarkable accuracy in answer detection and extraction, few works have considered returning a verbalized response to the user. Indeed, most of QA systems outputs over Knowledge Bases (KBs) are utterly bereft of any context. To this extent, more works progressively tackled the Answer Verbalization task (AV) which consists in generating a verbalized form of the answer. As a consequence, the user may benefit from a more contextualized response.

Recently, there have been few techniques proposed to perform surface realisation of a raw answer. With the lack of paired training data, Akermi et al. (2020) investigated an unsupervised method to obtain answer verbalizations for both English and French languages. An initial step was to first check whether the question marker (e.g. *Who, What*) could be *straightforwardly* substituted with the raw answer or not. For instance, with the question *"Who is the president of the U.S.?"*, its raw answer *"Joe Biden"* can directly replace the question marker *"who"* with the question mark substituted with a period. If this is not the case, the question is segmented into chunks based on the syntactic tree parsed with UDPipeFuture (Straka, 2018; Akermi et al., 2021). After defining the raw answer as a new chunk, all possible permutations of the chunks are collected. The most likely permutation is identified with a PLM such as GPT2 (Radford et al., 2019). Finally, Akermi et al. (2020) use BERT (Devlin et al., 2019) to find any possibly missing function words around the raw answer such as *a, an, to, with, in* etc. In spite of its appealing unsupervised mechanism, this method is computationally expensive because of the cost of estimating the likelihood of all (distinct) permutations. Moreover, the likelihood is computed with potential absent words which may jeopardize the final ranking of permutations.

Proceedings of the Workshop on Structured and Unstructured Knowledge Integration (SUKI), pages 47 - 54
July 14, 2022 ©2022 Association for Computational Linguistics

Following, multiple datasets were released to spur the community to apply end-to-end learning (Kacupaj et al., 2020, 2021a; Biswas et al., 2021). Kacupaj et al. (2021c) introduced VOGUE, an end-to-end model based on a dual encoder-decoder architecture. More precisely, the input question is encoded with a first Transformer encoder (Vaswani et al., 2017). On top of that, a logical form of the question is also encoded with an additional Transformer encoder. The logical form is a simplified representation of the question, similar to a query, inspired from Plepi et al. (2021) and Kacupaj et al. (2021b). Taking our aforementioned question example, its logical form is `find(president, U.S)`. During the decoding phase, VOGUE uses entities placeholders[1] for both the raw answer and the subject entity to generate an abstract version of the response. Following the previous example, the generated verbalization would be *"`[ANS]` is the president of `[ENT]`"*. In our work, we utilize a comparable mechanism fused with large-scaled pretrained models to leverage efficient transfer learning.

Specifically, our contribution is twofold:

- We propose a masked answer verbalization coupled with transfer learning to verbalize extracted answers over KBs. Placeholders are generated instead of the correct raw answer. This allows a better generalization and scalability of the model. Then, a post-processing step is applied which consists of replacing the placeholder with the raw answer.
- We provide a minor revision of the VANILLA dataset by correcting entity hallucinations in 5% of the verbalizations. We show evidence that erroneous references may be the culprit of 0.13% absolute median SacreBLEU drop in evaluation and up to 0.81 absolute median gain in SacreBLEU when trained on corrected training data.

2 Our Approach

In this section, we present our method based on transfer learning and masked generation. We consider an input question $X = \{x_1, x_2, \ldots, x_{N-1}, x_N\}$ with x_i the ith word and its raw answer $A = \{a_1, a_2, \ldots, a_{K-1}, a_K\}$ with a_j the jth word of the answer[2]. The goal is to generate a verbalized answer $Y = \{y_1, y_2, \ldots, y_{M-1}, y_M\}$ We model the generation of each token as a conditional θ-parameterized probability distribution. More precisely, we estimate θ such that $P_\theta(y_i|X, A, y_1, y_2, \ldots, y_{i-1})$ is maximized.

As mentioned in Dai and Le (2015), Howard and Ruder (2018) and Montella et al. (2020), NLG has significantly benefited from transfer learning and very large PLMs (Devlin et al., 2019; Radford et al., 2019). The generalization ability to unseen data has tremendously improved over the last decades due to the use of excessively large training corpora. As a consequence, we consider two recent PLMs for generation to leverage transfer learning:

- **BART** (Lewis et al., 2020) is based on a Transformer architecture (Vaswani et al., 2017). More specifically, its encoder and decoder correspond to BERT (Devlin et al., 2019) and to GPT (Radford et al., 2019), respectively. During training, BART is pretrained with a denoising objective. It consists in corrupting the input of the model (masking, reordering, etc) and to reconstruct the original, i.e. denoised, input.
- **T5** (Raffel et al., 2020) is similar to the Transformer-based model (Vaswani et al., 2017) with minor changes. For instance, as positional embeddings, a single scalar is added to the logits used for attention weights computation. Also, a simplified layer normalization is utilized. T5 is trained on multiple tasks at once such as question answering, language modeling, span extraction, paraphrasing, sentiment analysis, etc. To do so, all text processing tasks are cast in a text-to-text framework which allows to reuse the same model, loss function, optimizer and so on. Both input and target are textual content or transformed as text. Thus, for binary, numerical or categorical data types, T5 maps such format to strings. Moreover, a specificity of T5 is that the task is informed within the input thanks to a prefix, e.g. *"translate English to German:"* or *"summarize:"*. While finetuning, it is a good practice to reuse the same prefix as the downstream task for efficient transfer learning.

In order to verbalize the answer, a first step consists in encoding X with the encoder part of T5 or BART model. Then, the decoder part takes learned

[1] We use the term *placeholder* and *mask* interchangeably.

[2] The raw answer can be of multiple words.

representations to generate Y. In our case, a placeholder is generated in Y which will be replaced by the raw answer A as explained in next section.

2.1 Masked Answer Verbalization

As humans, our ability to generate a response is independent and agnostic to our own knowledge. For instance, given the question *"What is the capital of Ghana?"*, although the answer, i.e. *"Accra"*, might not be known, one is still able to generate the response *"The capital of Ghana is* `[ANSWER]`*"* where `[ANSWER]` stands for a placeholder of the correct raw answer. Therefore, this paradigm could remain when modeling any question answering system. This is a two-stage process. First, a template of the verbalized answer is generated. Secondly, we replace the mask with the corresponding raw answer, i.e. a single or several entities, of the input question. We are aware that this approach works especially well in English, but would require adjustment to other languages such as French or German because of gender agreement. However, several benefits can be pointed out. It alleviates the training of the model since it principally learns to generate templates. In addition, it avoids misspelling of entities during the generation. It has been shown that unseen entities are not handled properly by the generative system (Ferreira et al., 2020). This is further critical when a copy mechanism is not applied. On top of that, using placeholders reduces the complexity of the model by shrinking its vocabulary dimension (last layer). This is also significant regarding training time since a softmax layer is usually applied which is known to be time consuming.

3 Datasets

More and more efforts have been made to construct and annotate new QA datasets. However, most of proposed corpora do not include a well-formed and informative response. In fact, no verbalization of the retrieved answer is usually given. Only the raw answer acts as the final prediction which puts a curb on possible downstream generation task. To this end, we explore newly released datasets equipped with a natural language form of the response:

- **VQuAnDa** (Kacupaj et al., 2020) is based on the Large scale Complex Question Answering Dataset (LC-QuAD). VQuAnDa provides a set of 5000 *complex* questions with their SPARQL queries and their corresponding answer verbalization. A semi-automatic process is used to derive the answer verbalization of each question. The available templates of the questions in LC-QuAD dataset are paraphrased using strict rules (use of active voice, synonyms, order rearranging, etc.) to get natural response templates. Then, a second step consists in extracting raw answers from DBpedia using the SPARQL queries. In case that the number of retrieved answers is greater than 15, the list of answers is replaced with a single token `[answer]` to avoid long sequences. Lastly, entities and predicates are filled accordingly to generate the final verbalization. To ensure correctness, resulting verbalization are checked *manually* according to (Kacupaj et al., 2021a). There are totally 4000 and 1000 pairs for training and testing sets, respectively.

- **ParaQA** (Kacupaj et al., 2021a) extends VQuAnDa by proposing multiple verbalizations for each question. This paraphrasing task was done using different techniques such as back-translation. At least two verbalizations per questions are given, and up to 8 unique paraphrases are provided in some cases. Thus, more pairs in training set can be found for the same question. We record a total of 12,637 pairs in training. Note that the training and testing splits of ParaQA are different than VQuAnDa.

- **VANiLLa** (Biswas et al., 2021) is a compelling dataset due to its size. Covering more than 300 relations, it was built using a semi-automatic framework. First, direct questions with single entity as answer were extracted from the Complex Sequential Question Answering (CSQA) (Saha et al., 2018) and SimpleQuestions[3] Datasets. After clustering similar questions based on 4-grams, a template-based verbalization of a single instance of each cluster was manually annotated thanks to Amazon Mechanical Turk (AMT). Finally, a post-processing aims at using the resulting templates to infer the verbalization for other similar questions in corresponding clusters. Totally, VANiLLa gathers 85,732 and 21,434 pairs for training and testing.

[3]Available at `https://github.com/davidgolub/SimpleQA/tree/master/datasets/SimpleQuestions`

	Train	Test
VQuAnDa	4,000	1,000
ParaQA	12,637	1,000
VANiLLa	85,732	21,434

Table 1: Datasets Statistics

These datasets are therefore suitable for the response generation task. Nonetheless, because of the semi-automatic framework, these corpora are prone to errors as we will show in Section 4.4

4 Experiments

In our experiments, we provide empirical results on the introduced datasets in Section 3. In Section 4.2, we compare our transfer learning approach over the existing literature using T5 and BART embedded with a masking strategy. Then, we explore the advantage of placeholders in Section 4.3. Our inputs and outputs with and without our masking approach are depicted in Table 2.

4.1 Training Settings

We use the pretrained BART and T5 models from HuggingFace. For both PLMs, we use their base models, i.e. `facebook/bart-base` and `t5-base` configurations. The input questions and target responses are all lower-cased. Since no validation sets are provided regarding the official splits, we arbitrarily set our hyperparameters for all of our experiments and do not validate them. We choose to finetune models on 10 epochs using a batch size of 32. We use the cross entropy loss and Adam optimizer for optimization. The initial learning rates are set to 1.0×10^{-5} and 1.0×10^{-4} for BART and T5 respectively.[4] For T5, we prefix each question with the prefix *"question:"* as it has already been used during T5 pretraining for question-answering. During generation, we use a greedy decoding (no beam search or sampling is applied). For better reproducibility, our code is available at `https://github.com/Anonymous1911272/answerverbalization`.

4.2 Results

Evaluation of natural language remains a critical issue since it is difficult to automate. Besides, human annotations are usually costly and time-consuming. For fair comparison, we follow exactly the same evaluation protocol and metrics as Kacupaj et al. (2021c), using BLEU (on 4-grams) (Papineni et al., 2002) and METEOR (Banerjee and Lavie, 2005)[5]. Since our predicted verbalizations contain placeholders, we replace them with the raw answers included in the dataset. Therefore, our evaluation does not differ between unmasked approaches. Results on VQuAnDa, ParaQA and VANiLLa datasets are depicted in Table 3.

We can see that transfer learning methods *systematically* show best (bold) or second-to-best (underlined) performances on all datasets. This is not surprising as large pretraining has shown massive improvements over standard approaches. BART exhibits much better performances than T5 on VQuAnDa and ParaQA. On the contrary, T5 is slightly better on VANiLLa. We conjecture that BART is well-fitted to map question to its answer verbalization. Question and response usually share similar words, but in different orders and few words or preprosition could be missing to go from one to another. This exactly corresponds to the denoising objective on which BART has been pretrained. Therefore, the input question can be viewed as a noisy version of the answer verbalization from which BART attempts to reconstruct. Regardless, pretrained models on average results in 44.25%, 3.26% and 29.10% relative gain in BLEU over VOGUE on VQuAnDa, ParaQA and VANiLLa respectively. VOGUE nonetheless shows interesting results despite its size and no pretraining. This is also explained by the logical form of the question which boils down the question to a simple abstraction. Furthermore, we observe that the unsupervised strategy by Akermi et al. (2020) has strong shortcoming to compete with a basic RNN. Their method is sensitive to the syntax and length of the input question. The longer the question, the worst the generation. While the verbalizations in VQuAnDa and ParaQA are 17 tokens long on average, this might be the reason of low performances on these datasets. Moreover, unnatural questions, as included in VANiLLa, are not handled properly because of the use of PLMs to gauge the likelihood of permutations.

In the following, our interest lies in measuring the real gain of using placeholders.

[4] We witness divergence when learning rate is set to 1.0×10^{-4} for BART.

[5] Kacupaj et al. (2021c) average the BLEU and METEOR of each verbalization.

	Input	Output
w/o mask	*Who is the president of the U.S.?* [SEP] *J. Biden*	*The president of the U.S. is J. Biden.*
w/ mask	*Who is the president of the U.S.?*	*The president of the U.S. is* [ANSWER] .

Table 2: Examples of model input and output with and without placeholders. During evaluation, the placeholder is replaced with the raw answer *J. Biden*.

	BLEU ↑			METEOR ↑		
Models	VQuAnDa	ParaQA	VANiLLa	VQuAnDa	ParaQA	VANiLLa
RNN†	15.43	22.45	16.66	53.15	58.41	58.67
Transformer†	18.37	23.61	30.80	56.83	59.63	62.16
Akermi et al. (2020)	22.70	18.25	18.30	48.04	44.27	48.27
VOGUE†	28.76	<u>32.05</u>	35.46	67.21	**68.85**	65.04
T5 (masking)	<u>39.07</u>	30.62	**45.87**	<u>67.70</u>	59.81	**67.15**
BART (masking)	**43.90**	**35.57**	<u>45.69</u>	**71.92**	<u>65.40</u>	<u>66.71</u>

Table 3: Answer Verbalization Results. (†) results are taken from Kacupaj et al. (2021c).

		BLEU ↑	METEOR ↑	SacreBLEU ↑	Chrf++ ↑	TER ↓
T5	w/o mask	30.06	58.39	35.25	56.44	52.67
	w/ mask	**39.07**	**67.70**	**58.26**	**73.87**	**42.45**
BART	w/o mask	33.93	61.43	39.19	59.26	49.22
	w/ mask	**43.90**	**71.92**	**60.85**	**75.45**	**35.36**

Table 4: Results with and without placeholders on VQuAnDa.

		BLEU ↑	METEOR ↑	SacreBLEU ↑	Chrf++ ↑	TER ↓
T5	w/o mask	25.55	53.55	33.49	53.84	56.04
	w/ mask	**30.62**	**59.81**	**47.01**	**66.39**	**49.87**
BART	w/o mask	30.56	57.80	37.61	56.95	52.41
	w/ mask	**35.57**	**65.40**	**50.70**	**68.86**	**43.50**

Table 5: Results with and without placeholders on ParaQA.

		BLEU ↑	METEOR ↑	SacreBLEU ↑	Chrf++ ↑	TER ↓
T5	w/o mask	42.91	64.56	53.33	70.19	44.41
	w/ mask	**45.87**	**67.15**	**57.67**	**73.40**	**41.59**
Bart	w/o mask	43.14	65.13	54.16	71.36	43.99
	w/ mask	**45.69**	**66.71**	**57.41**	**73.07**	**42.00**

Table 6: Results with and without placeholders on VANiLLa.

4.3 To Mask or not to Mask?

In this section, we investigate the impact of using a masking mechanism. We conduct a comparative study between masked and non-masked generation.

To do so, we finetune BART and T5 with the same hyperparameters as previous experiments. For non-masked generation, the input question is concatenated with its raw answer. To differentiate question and answer, we make use of the separator token [SEP]. With this setting, models should learn to combine input question and input answer accordingly to form a grammatically correct verbalization. We adopt additional evaluation metric, i.e. SacreBLEU (Post, 2018), Chrf++ (Popović, 2015) and TER (Snover et al., 2006), yielding much fine-grained analysis. The experiment results for VQuAnDa, ParaQA and VANiLLa are shown in Table 4, 5 and 6.

On the three datasets, we observe that using a placeholder leads to systematic gain for all reported metrics. More importantly, the gap can be considerably significant when masking the raw answer.

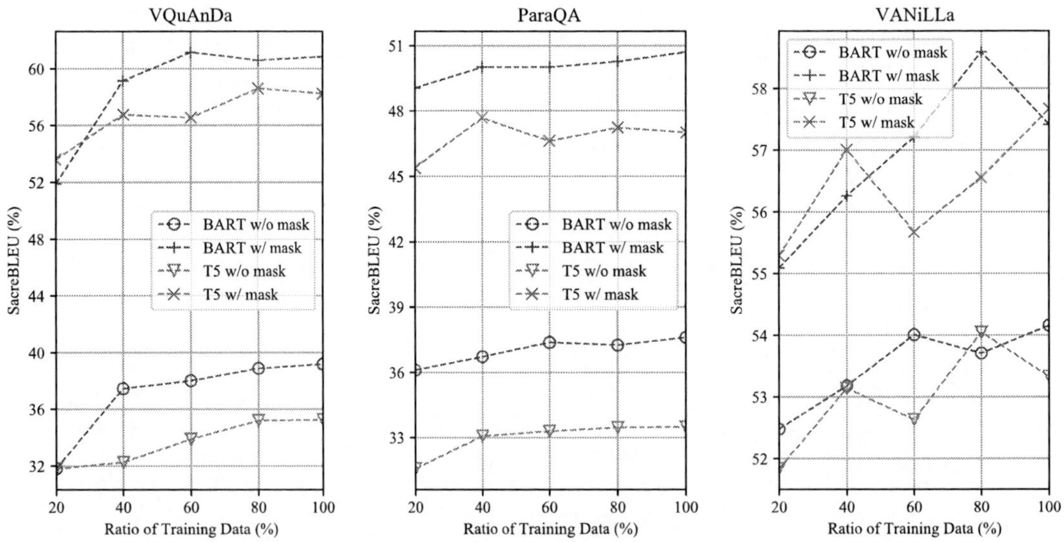

Figure 1: Tuning proportion of training data

		Test Set					Test Set	
		raw	corrected				raw	corrected
T5	w/o mask	53.33	**53.45**		T5	w/o mask	52.72	**53.58**
	w/ mask	57.67	**57.81**			w/ mask	57.48	**58.23**
BART	w/o mask	54.16	**54.30**		BART	w/o mask	54.96	**55.81**
	w/ mask	**57.41**	57.16			w/ mask	58.36	**59.13**

Table 7: SacreBLEU scores of T5 and BART trained on raw VANiLLa (left) and corrected VANiLLa (right)

For T5 and BART, we note 23.01%, 13.52%, 4.34% and 21.56%, 13.09%, 3.25% absolute gain in SacreBLEU for VQuAnDa, ParaQA and VANiLLa respectively. Thus, generating a more abstract verbalization alleviates the learning. Following, we inspect the effect of the size of training set. We thereby finetune BART and T5 on different (random) proportion of training data. We report SacreBLEU scores for each portion of training data in Fig. 1. At first glance, the gap between masked and non-masked generation remains very distinctive despite using less training data. We remark for T5 and BART about 23.09%, 13.81%, 3.44% and 21.65%, 13.00%, 3.40% absolute gain on average in SacreBLEU on VQuAnDa, ParaQA and VANiLLa while tuning amount of data fed to models. We observe that both masked and unmasked strategies keep increasing performances when new samples are given. Contrary to expectation, despite the use of placeholder, masked generation keeps benefiting of some significant performance leaps. For BART on VQuAnDa and ParaQA, SacreBLEU reaches a limit with only 40% of the training data in both configurations. On VANiLLa, models show much more variance, but a positive trend remains overall.

4.4 References are not Innocent

Semi-automatic dataset construction is a convenient yet effective technique to automatically generate sizeable corpora. Few handcrafted annotations are needed as initial seed. However, resulting samples are highly prone to errors or not natural. This remains a major drawback in the NLG community where the low quality or diversity of the available data jeopardize comparison between approaches. Within the VANiLLa dataset, we particularly reveal some verbalizations where the subject entity of the question differs with the subject entity of the reference. For example, given the question *"Which sex does Doris Miller belong to?"*, the assigned reference is *"Sterjo is a male"*, with *"Sterjo"* a hallucinated entity, which should be corrected with *"Doris Miller"*. Those hallucinated entities in gold references especially occur with specific and redundant entities (e.g. *"Sterjo"*). We assume the semi-automatic pipeline to be the culprit of such mismatch. Fortunately, those errors can be corrected automatically since the subject entity of each question is explicitly inquired in the original dataset. We identified 12 repeated hallucinated entities over the whole training set of VANiLLa. We thus interchange erroneous entities with correct ones. This stands for 5% for each of the training and testing set. The quality and diversity of references was proved to be at the core of variations of automated metrics outcomes (Freitag et al., 2020). Errors in references directly jeopardize resulting performances of models. Indeed, good predictions might be rated as bad quality while being correct. Furthermore, automatic metrics are critically sensitive to any changes in chosen words in target verbalization. We hence investigate the shift in reported results with corrected references. Precisely, we finetune T5 and BART with same hyperparameters as previously mentioned in Section 4.1. We train and evaluate models on the original VANiLLa dataset (*"Raw"*) and the corrected version (*"Corrected"*). The SacreBLEU scores are given in Table 7.

With only 5% of corrections in both training and testing sets, we record small improvements in SacreBLEU. Although the increases are relatively insignificant, those results clearly indicates that the quality of the references is crucial to precisely assess models performances. More and more works are competing in improving those metrics. Several contributions in generation considered slight improvements as predominance of their approaches over previous methods. However, we show in Table 7 that evaluating models on a corrected version lead to different results that are not systematically better. In contrast, when trained on much higher quality samples, results on corrected testing examples exhibits more important gain as seen in Table 7. The absolute median gain reaches 0.81 SacreBLEU with a cleaner training set while barely 0.13 with the standard training set. As a consequence, it is hard to compare and to draw any conclusions between models on noisy datasets. It is then important to raise awareness toward automatic dataset construction.

5 Conclusion

We proposed to verbalize answers usually returned by any question-answering system from a structured knowledge base. We combined the advantages of transfer learning and masked generation. We compared our strategies with and without masks using T5 and BART. We showed that using massively pretrained models with answer placeholders alleviates the learning and led to unprecedented results on VQuAnDa, ParaQA and VANiLLa datasets. Furthermore, we revealed multiple redundant entity hallucinations in the VANiLLa dataset. By automatically correcting 5% of them, we observed shifts in performances. This further demonstrates the limitation of automatic metrics when references are not reliable.

References

Imen Akermi, Johannes Heinecke, and Frédéric Herledan. 2020. Transformer based natural language generation for question-answering. In *Proceedings of the 3rd International Workshop on Natural Language Generation from the Semantic Web (WebNLG+)*, page 349–359, Dublin, Ireland (Virtual). Association for Computational Linguistics.

Imen Akermi, Johannes Heinecke, and Frédéric Herledan. 2021. Génération automatique de texte en langage naturel pour les systèmes de questions-réponses. *Traitement Automatique des Langues*, 62(1):13–37.

Satanjeev Banerjee and Alon Lavie. 2005. METEOR: An automatic metric for MT evaluation with improved correlation with human judgments. In *Proceedings of the ACL Workshop on Intrinsic and Extrinsic Evaluation Measures for Machine Translation and/or Summarization*, pages 65–72, Ann Arbor, Michigan. Association for Computational Linguistics.

Debanjali Biswas, Mohnish Dubey, Md Rashad Al Hasan Rony, and Jens Lehmann. 2021. Vanilla: Verbalized answers in natural language at large scale. arXiv:2105.11407.

Andrew M Dai and Quoc V Le. 2015. Semi-supervised sequence learning. In *Advances in Neural Information Processing Systems*, volume 28. Curran Associates, Inc.

Jacob Devlin, Ming-Wei Chang, Kenton Lee, and Kristina Toutanova. 2019. BERT: Pre-training of Deep Bidirectional Transformers for Language Understanding. In *Proceedings of the 2019 Conference of the North American Chapter of the Association for Computational Linguistics: Human Language Technologies, Volume 1 (Long and Short Papers)*, pages 4171–4186, Stroudsburg, PA, USA. Association for Computational Linguistics.

Thiago Castro Ferreira, Claire Gardent, Nikolai Ilinykh, Chris Van Der Lee, Simon Mille, Diego Moussallem, and Anastasia Shimorina. 2020. The 2020 Bilingual,

Bi-Directional WebNLG+ Shared Task Overview and Evaluation Results (WebNLG+ 2020). In *Proceedings of the 3rd International Workshop on Natural Language Generation from the Semantic Web (WebNLG+)*, Dublin/Virtual, Ireland.

Markus Freitag, David Grangier, and Isaac Caswell. 2020. BLEU might be guilty but references are not innocent. In *Proceedings of the 2020 Conference on Empirical Methods in Natural Language Processing (EMNLP)*, pages 61–71, Online. Association for Computational Linguistics.

Jeremy Howard and Sebastian Ruder. 2018. Universal language model fine-tuning for text classification. In *Proceedings of the 56th Annual Meeting of the Association for Computational Linguistics (Volume 1: Long Papers)*, pages 328–339, Melbourne, Australia. Association for Computational Linguistics.

Endri Kacupaj, Barshana Banerjee, Kuldeep Singh, and Jens Lehmann. 2021a. Paraqa: A question answering dataset with paraphrase responses for single-turn conversation. In *ESWC 2021*, pages 598–613.

Endri Kacupaj, Joan Plepi, Kuldeep Singh, Harsh Thakkar, Jens Lehmann, and Maria Maleshkova. 2021b. Conversational question answering over knowledge graphs with transformer and graph attention networks. In *Proceedings of the 16th Conference of the European Chapter of the Association for Computational Linguistics: Main Volume*, pages 850–862, Online. Association for Computational Linguistics.

Endri Kacupaj, Shyamnath Premnadh, Kuldeep Singh, Jens Lehmann, and Maria Maleshkova. 2021c. Vogue: Answer verbalization through multi-task learning. In *Machine Learning and Knowledge Discovery in Databases. Research Track*, pages 563–579, Cham. Springer International Publishing.

Endri Kacupaj, Hamid Zafar, Jens Lehmann, and Maria Maleshkova. 2020. Vquanda: Verbalization question answering dataset. In *The Semantic Web*, pages 531–547, Cham. Springer International Publishing.

Mike Lewis, Yinhan Liu, Naman Goyal, Marjan Ghazvininejad, Abdelrahman Mohamed, Omer Levy, Veselin Stoyanov, and Luke Zettlemoyer. 2020. BART: Denoising sequence-to-sequence pre-training for natural language generation, translation, and comprehension. In *Proceedings of the 58th Annual Meeting of the Association for Computational Linguistics*, pages 7871–7880, Online. Association for Computational Linguistics.

Sebastien Montella, Betty Fabre, Tanguy Urvoy, Johannes Heinecke, and Lina Rojas-Barahona. 2020. Denoising pre-training and data augmentation strategies for enhanced RDF verbalization with transformers. In *Proceedings of the 3rd International Workshop on Natural Language Generation from the Semantic Web (WebNLG+)*, pages 89–99, Dublin, Ireland (Virtual). Association for Computational Linguistics.

Kishore Papineni, Salim Roukos, Todd Ward, and Wei-Jing Zhu. 2002. Bleu: a method for automatic evaluation of machine translation. In *Proceedings of the 40th Annual Meeting of the Association for Computational Linguistics*, pages 311–318, Philadelphia, Pennsylvania, USA. Association for Computational Linguistics.

Joan Plepi, Endri Kacupaj, Kuldeep Singh, Harsh Thakkar, and Jens Lehmann. 2021. Context transformer with stacked pointer networks for conversational question answering over knowledge graphs. In *The Semantic Web*, pages 356–371, Cham. Springer International Publishing.

Maja Popović. 2015. chrF: character n-gram F-score for automatic MT evaluation. In *Proceedings of the Tenth Workshop on Statistical Machine Translation*, pages 392–395, Lisbon, Portugal. Association for Computational Linguistics.

Matt Post. 2018. A call for clarity in reporting BLEU scores. In *Proceedings of the Third Conference on Machine Translation: Research Papers*, pages 186–191, Brussels, Belgium. Association for Computational Linguistics.

Alec Radford, Jeffrey Wu, Rewon Child, David Luan, Dario Amodei, and Ilya Sutskever. 2019. Language Models are Unsupervised Multitask Learners. https://openai.com/blog/better-language-models/.

Colin Raffel, Noam Shazeer, Adam Roberts, Katherine Lee, Sharan Narang, Michael Matena, Yanqi Zhou, Wei Li, and Peter J. Liu. 2020. Exploring the limits of transfer learning with a unified text-to-text transformer. *Journal of Machine Learning Research*, 21(140):1–67.

Amrita Saha, Vardaan Pahuja, Mitesh M. Khapra, Karthik Sankaranarayanan, and Sarath Chandar. 2018. Complex sequential question answering: Towards learning to converse over linked question answer pairs with a knowledge graph. arXiv:1801.10314.

Matthew Snover, Bonnie Dorr, Rich Schwartz, Linnea Micciulla, and John Makhoul. 2006. A study of translation edit rate with targeted human annotation. In *Proceedings of the 7th Conference of the Association for Machine Translation in the Americas: Technical Papers*, pages 223–231, Cambridge, Massachusetts, USA. Association for Machine Translation in the Americas.

Milan Straka. 2018. UDPipe 2.0 Prototype at CoNLL 2018 UD Shared Task. In *Proceedings of the CoNLL 2018 Shared Task: Multilingual Parsing from Raw Text to Universal Dependencies*, pages 197–207, Brussels. Association for Computational Linguistics.

Ashish Vaswani, Noam Shazeer, Niki Parmar, Jakob Uszkoreit, Llion Jones, Aidan N Gomez, Łukasz Kaiser, and Illia Polosukhin. 2017. Attention is all you need. In *Advances in Neural Information Processing Systems*, volume 30. Curran Associates, Inc.

Knowledge Transfer between Structured and Unstructured Sources for Complex Question Answering

Lingbo Mo[*]**, Zhen Wang**[*]**, Jie Zhao, Huan Sun**
The Ohio State University
{mo.169,wang.9215,zhao.1359,sun.397}@osu.edu

Abstract

Multi-hop question answering (QA) combines multiple pieces of evidence to search for the correct answer. Reasoning over a text corpus (TextQA) and/or a knowledge base (KBQA) has been extensively studied and led to distinct system architectures. However, knowledge transfer between such two QA systems has been under-explored. Research questions like what knowledge is transferred or whether the transferred knowledge can help answer over one source using another one, are yet to be answered. In this paper, therefore, we study the knowledge transfer of multi-hop reasoning between structured and unstructured sources. We first propose a unified QA framework named SIMULTQA to enable knowledge transfer and bridge the distinct supervisions from KB and text sources. Then, we conduct extensive analyses to explore how knowledge is transferred by leveraging the pre-training and fine-tuning paradigm. We focus on the low-resource fine-tuning to show that pre-training SIMULTQA on one source can substantially improve its performance on the other source. More fine-grained analyses on transfer behaviors reveal the types of transferred knowledge and transfer patterns. We conclude with insights into how to construct better QA datasets and systems to exploit knowledge transfer for future work.[1]

1 Introduction

Structured knowledge source, such as Knowledge Base (KB) and unstructured knowledge source, such as text corpus, are arguably the most popular sources for complex question answering (CQA). Multi-hop KB based question answering (KBQA) systems translate questions to logical forms to be executed over a KB for finding answers (Talmor and Berant, 2018; Maheshwari et al., 2019; Lan and Jiang, 2020; Gu et al., 2020; Das et al., 2021; Ye et al., 2021), while text based QA (TextQA) systems leverage large text corpora to retrieve paragraphs and extract answer spans for complex questions (Yang et al., 2018; Qi et al., 2019; Asai et al., 2020; Dhingra et al., 2020; Zhu et al., 2021).

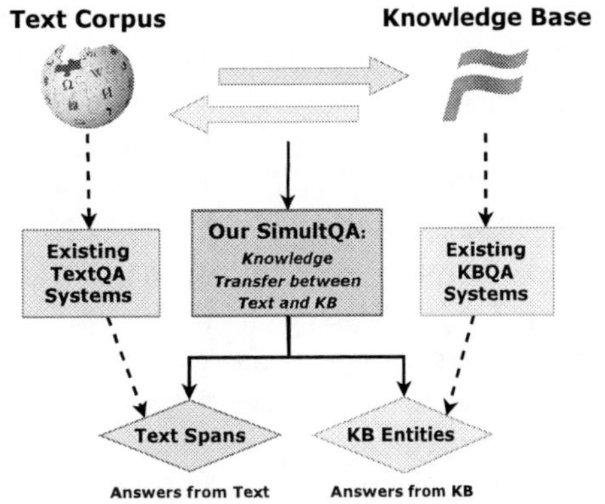

Figure 1: To facilitate knowledge transfer between structured and unstructured sources, we develop a unified framework SIMULTQA that can leverage supervisions from both sources to answer complex questions.

However, despite the impressive performance of separate KBQA and TextQA systems, it is not quite clear to the community whether a system trained on one source can be transferred and beneficial to question answering over another source. Inspired by the general transfer learning in NLP by pre-trained language models (PLMs) (Radford et al., 2018; Devlin et al., 2019; Raffel et al., 2020), it is important to study this research problem systematically and thoroughly for the following reasons. First, given the heterogeneity of structured and unstructured sources, it is desirable to build a unified reasoning module to work on both text and KB and combine different source-specific supervisions. Second, transfer learning has shown to boost the performance on low-resource domains, and it would be practically useful to leverage annotated datasets on one source for CQA on the other source, especially when human annotations are expensive to create new multi-hop QA datasets. Third, it is

[*]Equal contribution
[1]Code and data are available at https://github.com/Stefan1220/SimultQA

Proceedings of the Workshop on Structured and Unstructured Knowledge Integration (SUKI), pages 55 - 66
July 14, 2022

also critical to investigate what kind of knowledge can be transferred, which can inspire future CQA dataset creation and system design.

One major obstacle in such an investigation for knowledge transfer between structured and unstructured sources is the disparity of them and their specifically designed QA systems as we mentioned earlier. For instance, KB is highly structured and curated where complex query functions can be executed, while text data is unstructured and noisier, leading to quite distinct QA systems. One relevant line of research is HybridQA that tries to leverage multiple sources for QA (Mihaylov and Frank, 2018; Sun et al., 2018, 2019; Min et al., 2019; Oguz et al., 2020; Shi et al., 2021). To operate their single model on both KB and text, these methods primarily convert distinct sources into similar data format, e.g., merge text and KB by entity linking, which sacrifices unique characteristics of each source to some extent and makes it harder to investigate knowledge transfer as sources are entangled together. Thus, typical HybridQA methods are not suitable for studying knowledge transfer problem.

In this paper, *our first contribution* is proposing a unified CQA framework to enable knowledge transfer between structured and unstructured sources. The proposed framework, SIMULTQA, could perform multi-hop reasoning over text and KB simultaneously by collecting reasoning paths from either text or KB, then rerank paths to select the best one for generating the answer. There are several new and desirable properties of SIMULTQA. First, SIMULTQA unifies the recent advanced KBQA (Luo et al., 2018; Lan and Jiang, 2020) and TextQA (Chen et al., 2017; Asai et al., 2020) systems seamlessly, which preserves their unique strengths maximally to handle various reasoning types. Second, SIMULTQA can utilize distinct supervisions from both sources, which has the potential to combine both KBQA and TextQA datasets for a unified training. Last but not least, since SIMULTQA can be applied to any source, we can pre-train it on KB and fine-tune it on text and vice versa, which makes it easier to quantify transfer effect brought by the pre-training on a different source. In summary, despite the framework design looks straightforward, we are the first to unify two seemingly distinct CQA systems and study knowledge transfer between two sources for CQA.

With SIMULTQA that enables knowledge transfer, *our second contribution* is to systematically analyze the transfer behavior to help us deeply understand the nature of the multi-hop reasoning process in KB and Text. We apply our methodology to CWQ (Talmor and Berant, 2018) and HotpotQA (Yang et al., 2018), which are arguably the most popular dataset in KB and text source, and are representative enough to cover most of the reasoning types on KB and text. We first show that pre-training on one source can consistently improve the fine-tuning performance on the other one in the low-resource setting, indicating future data-hungry QA systems can be boosted by pre-training on another disparate source, especially when human annotation is expensive. More interestingly, further fine-grained analyses attempt to reveal sources of performance gain and find out what knowledge is transferred. We mainly investigate three aspects, reasoning types, reasoning hops and question similarity. We find that despite KB and text sources are quite disparate, SIMULTQA still find ways to transfer knowledge by learning a shared semantic space for the reasoning and a high-level understanding beyond distinct surface forms of reasoning paths. In addition, we study a more challenging transfer setting where we seek to use text reasoning to answer KB-based questions[2] and vice versa. Promising results are obtained by using text knowledge to help KB questions highlighting the expressiveness of text corpus. We conclude that knowledge transfer between structured and unstructured sources is an intriguing direction to combine the strengths of KBQA and TextQA systems and to use data from one source to boost QA on the other. To the best of our knowledge, this paper is the first to study knowledge transfer between KB- and text-based CQA in a quantitative and systematic manner.

2 Related Work

Complex Question Answering. There has been a long history of QA models to answer simple questions (Berant et al., 2013; Rajpurkar et al., 2016; Chen et al., 2017; Wang et al., 2018; Lee et al., 2018; Yang et al., 2019; Karpukhin et al., 2020). More recent attention has focused on answering complex questions, which requires a multi-hop reasoning process (Yang et al., 2018; Fang et al., 2020). For example, some of them target questions that can be answered using multiple text paragraphs as evidences (Das et al., 2018; Qi et al., 2019; Feldman and El-Yaniv, 2019; Asai et al., 2020), while

[2]We refer to questions originally from KBQA/TextQA datasets as KB-based/text-based questions in this paper.

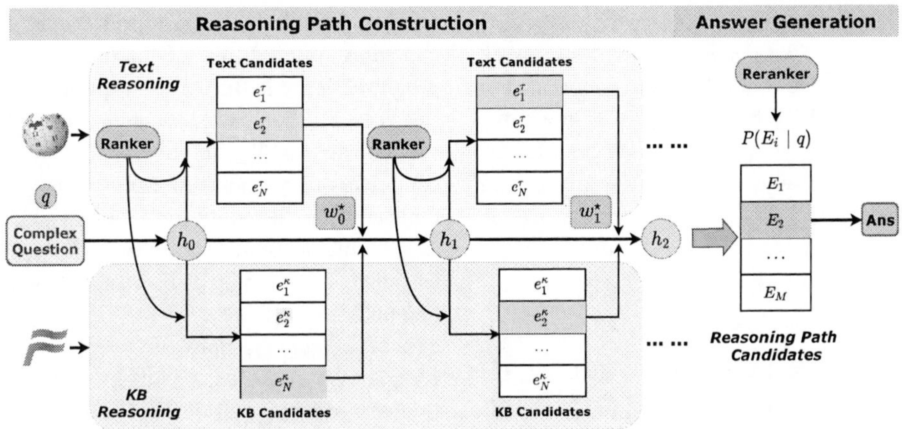

Figure 2: Overview of SIMULTQA Framework. There are two stages including constructing reasoning path from either text or KB, and path reranking for the answer generation. In the inference time, the reasoning can be performed simultaneously over text and KB source to find the final answer.

some existing KBQA works (Bao et al., 2016; Luo et al., 2018; Chen et al., 2019; Lan et al., 2019; Lan and Jiang, 2020) studied how to answer questions by iteratively chaining multiple knowledge base relations into the evidence path. Our proposed framework unifies these two recent trends of CQA frameworks in text and KB to study knowledge transfer between them.

Hybrid Question Answering. HybridQA is a line of QA research that also studies different knowledge sources (e.g., text articles, Web tables, knowledge bases) for answering questions (Mihaylov and Frank, 2018; Sun et al., 2018, 2019; Xiong et al., 2019; Min et al., 2019; Oguz et al., 2020; Chen et al., 2020a,b). This line of work typically requires extra human efforts to merge hybrid data for later complex modeling, for example, linking text paragraphs to KB by entity linking or universal schema (Das et al., 2017; Sun et al., 2018, 2019) or converting KB edges to plain text (Oguz et al., 2020), which is not needed in SIMULTQA. Their major motivation is to unify data formats for text and KB and construct a more comprehensive knowledge space, which is orthogonal to our motivation of studying knowledge transfer between intact knowledge space of text and KB.

Transfer Learning in NLP. In the last few years, NLP has witnessed the emergence of several transfer learning techniques, and their effectiveness of constantly improving state-of-the-art on a wide range of NLP tasks. Traditional transfer learning techniques (Pan and Yang, 2009) include multi-task learning, domain adaptation, etc (Liu et al., 2019; Clark et al., 2019; Ruder et al., 2019). More recently, fine-tuning PLMs has become the de facto standard for transferring knowledge among NLP tasks (Peters et al., 2018; Radford et al., 2018; Devlin et al., 2019; Raffel et al., 2020). In this paper, we study knowledge transfer between structured and unstructured sources in CQA task and use BERT models as the backbone of our approach.

3 SIMULTQA Framework

SIMULTQA is a unified framework for multi-hop reasoning to incorporate both KB and text sources. It consists of two stages, iteratively reasoning and final reranking, which can be trained with supervisions from both sources.

3.1 Reasoning Path Construction

CQA requires a multi-hop reasoning process to derive the answer. For KBQA, the reasoning is to traverse the knowledge graph for multi-steps based on generated queries from the question, while for TextQA, it is to collect multiple documents from a text corpus. We consolidate both by iteratively searching for evidence from each source and construct the reasoning path at the end. The key formulation is we treat each step as a ranking problem and train the model to select the most appropriate document/ KB query graph from text corpus/ knowledge graph that can answer the complex question.

Formally, at time step t, $(t \geq 1)$, we are given the complex question q, a pool of candidate evidences, $e_i \in \{e_1, ..., e_N\}$, and the hidden state h_{t-1} from previous step. We first encode them by the BERT [CLS] token representation to get the contextual embedding $\mathbf{w}_i$ for each candidate e_i. Then, we calculate the probability of e_i to be selected in current step by feeding $\mathbf{w}_i$ to a fully-connected layer. We denote text evidence as $e_i^{\mathcal{T}}$ which is a sequence of tokens from a document in the text corpus. For KB evidence, following previous work (Lan and Jiang, 2020), each candidate is "serialized" into a sequence of relation tokens and denoted as $e_i^{\mathcal{K}}$. The scoring process at t-th step is defined as follows:

$$\mathbf{w}_i^{\mathcal{T}} = \text{BERT}_{[\text{CLS}]}([q; e_i^{\mathcal{T}}]), \quad (1)$$

$$\mathbf{w}_i^{\mathcal{K}} = \text{BERT}_{[\text{CLS}]}([q; e_i^{\mathcal{K}}]), \quad (2)$$

$$P_t^{\mathcal{T}}(e_i^{\mathcal{T}}|q) = \text{FC}(\mathbf{w}_i^{\mathcal{T}}, \mathbf{h}_t) \in [0, 1], \quad (3)$$

$$P_t^{\mathcal{K}}(e_i^{\mathcal{K}}|q) = \text{FC}(\mathbf{w}_i^{\mathcal{K}}, \mathbf{h}_t) \in [0, 1], \quad (4)$$

where $[q; e_i]$ represents the concatenation of the question and evidence separated by [SEP] token. We simply choose a Recurrent Neural Network (RNN), and h_t is calculated to model the sequential multi-hop reasoning process as follows:

$$\mathbf{h}_t = \text{RNN}(\mathbf{h}_{t-1}, \mathbf{w}_{t-1}^*) \in \mathbb{R}^d \quad (5)$$

where $\mathbf{w}_{t-1}^*$ encodes the ground-truth evidence in previous step for $t > 1$ during training and $\mathbf{h}_0$ will be a free parameterized vector to be initialized randomly, when $t = 1$. During inference, evidences will be dynamically inferred based on the results from previous step. To encourage knowledge transfer, we share the parameters for the recurrent module and BERT model (as well as the answer generation module that will be introduced later) for KB and text source, which will be jointly optimized. We next introduce how to generate high-quality candidate pools for each step.

Generate Text Candidates. Following previous methods (Chen et al., 2017), for a given complex question and a large text corpus (e.g., Wikipedia), we leverage TF-IDF based methods to retrieve top-K documents with the tri-gram hashing techniques. For the iterative process, we reuse TF-IDF method to retrieve candidates in next step combining the complex question and the previous retrieved document. Moreover, since TF-IDF methods mainly consider the lexical matching, there are several advanced approaches that can be explored to extend the reasoning path, such as meta-info based (e.g., entity links, hyperlinks (Nie et al., 2019; Asai et al., 2020)), search engine (Qi et al., 2019, 2020), dense retrieval (Xiong et al., 2021). We consider hyperlinks (Asai et al., 2020) in this work and leave more sophisticated methods to future work.

Generate KB Candidates. We follow recent advanced staged query generation methods (Yih et al., 2015; Luo et al., 2018; Lan and Jiang, 2020) to generate candidates and perform KB reasoning. As shown in Figure 2, the KB module starts from a grounded entity in the complex question and identifies core relation paths[3] as candidates with necessary constraints. We iteratively generate and rank candidate query graphs in each step based on the topic entity or the entity from the last step.

With the iterative ranking in each step, we can establish the reasoning chain as a sequence of documents, $E^{\mathcal{T}} = [e_1^{\mathcal{T}}, ..., e_k^{\mathcal{T}}]$ for TextQA and a sequence of query graphs, $E^{\mathcal{K}} = [e_1^{\mathcal{K}}, ..., e_k^{\mathcal{K}}]$ for KBQA. We score each path by the multiplication of probability of each selected evidence as $P(e_1|q) \cdot ... \cdot P(e_k|q)$ and use beam search to produce top-M reasoning paths $\{E_1, ..., E_M\}$ for the final answer generation.

3.2 Reranking and Answer Generation

Given a complex question q and several reasoning paths $\{E_1, ...E_M\}$ from the previous component, we rerank the paths based on how likely they can answer the question. We use another BERT [CLS] token representation to encode the reasoning path E_i with a fully connected model to output the probability of choosing E_i as follows:

$$\mathbf{v}_i = \text{BERT}_{[\text{CLS}]}([q, \{e_{i1}, ..., e_{ik}\}]), \quad (6)$$

$$P(E_i|q) = \text{FC}(\mathbf{v}_i) \in [0, 1] \quad (7)$$

After the reasoning path reranking, our system allows the KB reasoning path and text reasoning path to be handled differently. This reflects the advantage of our system to combine the strength of both KBQA and textQA as discussed earlier. Since KB is structured, we can directly execute the complete query graph in the knowledge graph to get the answers. For question answering with textual evidence chains in particular, another *reader* component is employed to select the text spans that are the final answer based on the top-ranked path.

3.3 Training and Inference

We leverage the annotated document labels from HotpotQA dataset to train the reasoning path construction and reranking modules. For CWQ dataset, we split the golden complex logic form into sub-queries by defining the sub-query to be composed of head/tail entities along with one relation or two relations with CVT type node. Constraint relations are also added to the connected sub-queries. The

[3]As in (Lan and Jiang, 2020), we allow the relation to be a single predicate or two predicates connected through a CVT node designed for a multi-argument relation.

sub-queries are treated as supervisions in each reasoning step as well as the path reranking module. Note that it is now the standard way to train robust CQA systems by leveraging full supervision in each hop. We leave utilizing distantly weak supervisions for training to future work. In each step of reasoning module, the loss functions for KB and text are defined as follows:

$$L_t^{\mathcal{T}} = -\log P(e_t^{\mathcal{T}}|q) - \sum_{\widetilde{e^{\mathcal{T}}} \in C_t^{\mathcal{T}}} \log(1 - P(\widetilde{e^{\mathcal{T}}}|q)) \quad (8)$$

$$L_t^{\mathcal{K}} = -\log P(e_t^{\mathcal{K}}|q) - \sum_{\widetilde{e^{\mathcal{K}}} \in C_t^{\mathcal{K}}} \log(1 - P(\widetilde{e^{\mathcal{K}}}|q)) \quad (9)$$

where $C_t^{\mathcal{T}}$ and $C_t^{\mathcal{K}}$ are negative samples. For text, we follow previous work (Asai et al., 2020) to generate lexically and semantically similar negative samples based on TF-IDF as well as hyperlinks. For KB, we treat all query graphs other than the golden one in the same step as negative samples.

In terms of reranking reasoning paths for KB and text, we reuse the previous supervisions to train a ranker model (Eqn. 7) for selecting the correct path with the loss function as follows:

$$L_{\text{rank}}^{\mathcal{T}} = -\sum_i y_i^{\mathcal{T}} \cdot \log(P(E_i^{\mathcal{T}}|q)) \quad (10)$$

$$L_{\text{rank}}^{\mathcal{K}} = -\sum_i y_i^{\mathcal{K}} \cdot \log(P(E_i^{\mathcal{K}}|q)) \quad (11)$$

where $y_i^{\mathcal{T}}$ and $y_i^{\mathcal{K}}$ are the assigned labels for the golden path of i-th sample from two sources. We also design negative samples for reasoning paths by replacing the golden evidence in one of k hops.

4 Knowledge Transfer Experiments

We focus on investigating knowledge transfer between structured and unstructured sources in this paper, though the proposed SIMULTQA can be applied to any open-domain CQA datasets. We seek to answer three research questions (RQs):

- **RQ1**: Can the knowledge learned on one source help the QA performance on another one? (§4.2)
- **RQ2**: What kind of knowledge has been transferred between KB and text? (§4.3)
- **RQ3**: Can knowledge transfer help answer questions by both sources? (§4.4)

4.1 Experimental Setup

Choice of Datasets. Investigating knowledge transfer between text and KB requires at least one dataset from each source. Without losing the generality, we choose Wikipedia and Freebase as the source for text and KB respectively, and select their arguably the most representative CQA dataset to cover the majority of reasoning types. We leave applying SIMULTQA to other domain-specific sources and datasets as future work.

The selected large-scale KB dataset is Complex WebQuestions (CWQ) (Talmor and Berant, 2018) that consists of around 27K/3.5K/3.5K samples for train/dev/test. The text dataset is HotpotQA (Yang et al., 2018) that consists of around 90K/7.4K/7.4K samples for train/dev/test. For both datasets, we focus on the most practical setting, which is the open-domain QA, meaning that the model needs to reason over the entire knowledge space for answering the question.

Implementation Details. We adopt pre-trained BERT models (Devlin et al., 2019) using the uncased base configuration (768-hidden) for our reasoning path construction and reranking module. We follow Graph Retriever (Asai et al., 2020) and use their pre-trained whole word masking uncased large configuration (1024-hidden) for the reader. During the process of reasoning path construction, we set the number of negative examples along with the gold example as 30, set the number of hops as 2, and use beam search when doing the inference. Beam size is set as 5 for CWQ and 9 for HotpotQA.

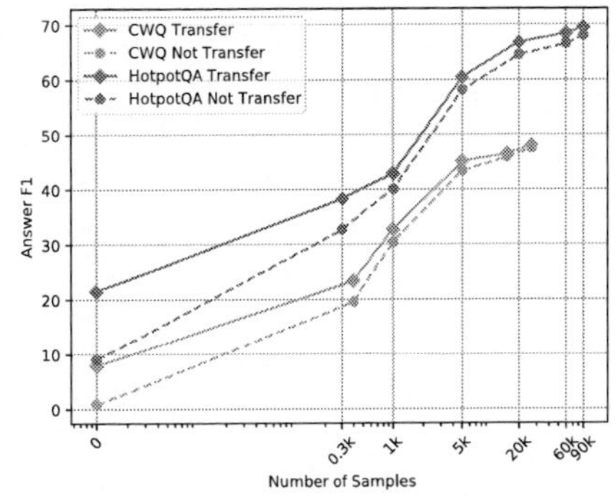

Figure 3: Pre-training and fine-tuning experiments on CWQ and HotpotQA datasets. We first pre-train SIMULTQA on one source with the full dataset, then fine-tune it on another one with various sizes of samples.

4.2 RQ1: Quantitative measurement

Pre-training and Fine-tuning. A straightforward way to investigate the effect of knowledge transfer between text and KB is to leverage the pre-training and fine-tuning paradigm, where we first pre-train SIMULTQA on one source and fine-tune it on another one. The transfer effect then can be measured by the performance difference with and without the pre-training stage. Furthermore, to demonstrate the transfer effect carefully, we focus on the low-

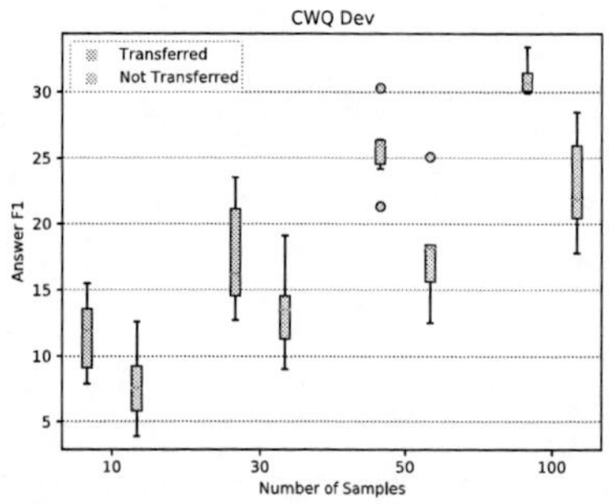

Figure 4: Few-shot experiments on CWQ dataset. Boxes extends from the first quartile to the third quartile of the samples, and lines inside boxes mark the medians.

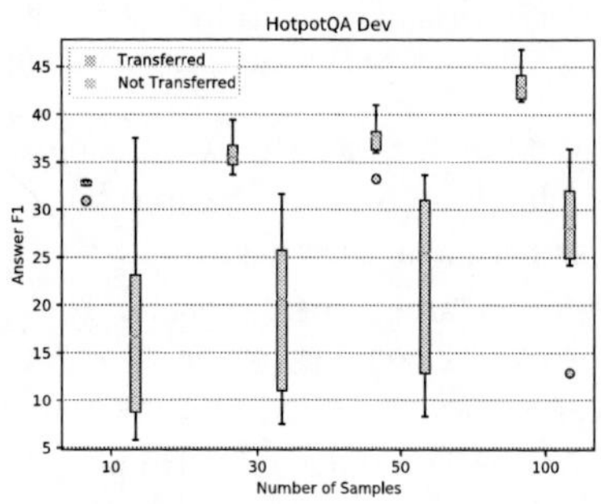

Figure 5: Few-shot experiments on HotpotQA dataset.

resource setting where we increasingly add more samples for the fine-tuning. Note that we only pre-train and fine-tune the first stage of SIMULTQA, which is the retriever, because this is the most important module for multi-hop reasoning.

Transfer Text Knowledge to KB. We show the fine-tuning performance in Figure 3, where we can see that pre-training SIMULTQA on text dataset can consistently improve the performance on KB dataset, especially when the fine-tuning data is limited. Specifically, when there is no fine-tuning data for KB (zero-shot transfer), text pre-training achieves about 8 F1 score on CWQ already, meaning that text knowledge can greatly help the QA model on KB. We also notice that when a large number of KB samples are available, the transfer effect becomes less prominent, possibly due to the model begins overfitting KB-specific features.

To further demonstrate the transfer effect on low-resource setting, we conduct few-shot experiments by randomly sampling only a handful of samples for fine-tuning. We sample five times to reduce the randomness of few-shot samples and results are shown in Figure 4. We can see the transfer effect from text to KB more clearly, and this finding can be leveraged to boost the performance of KBQA in low-data region when human annotations are

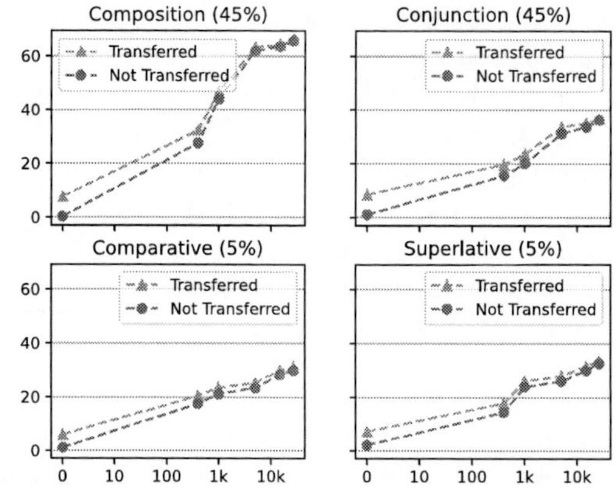

Figure 6: Analysis of reasoning types in CWQ. Numbers in parentheses are percentages of types.

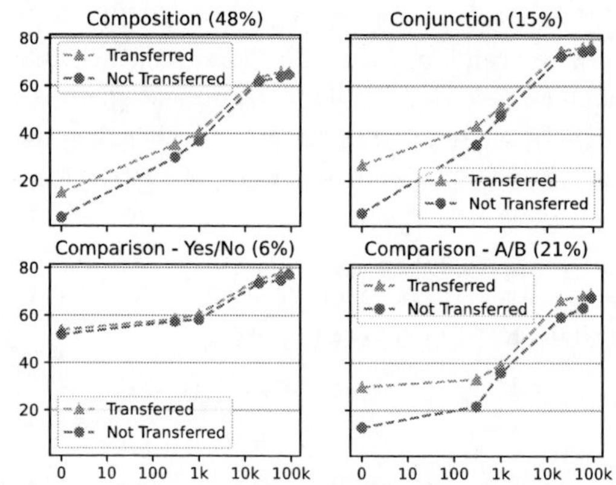

Figure 7: Analysis of reasoning types in HotpotQA. Numbers in parentheses are percentages of types.

expensive to collect over domain-specific KBs.

Transfer KB Knowledge to Text. Figure 3 shows the pre-training on KB also provides performance boost for fine-tuning on text domain in the low-resource setting. In zero-shot transfer, pre-training on KB brings about 12.5 F1 improvement, which verifies that KB knowledge can also help answer text-based questions. Moreover, few-shot experiments in Figure 5 demonstrate the transfer effect when < 100 text-based samples are available. We notice that the variance of few-shot experiments is greatly reduced by the pre-training, indicating another potential useful transfer effect may be to help reduce the instability in the few-shot learning. Meanwhile, we conduct error analysis for both CWQ and HotpotQA respectively in Table 2.

4.3 RQ2: What has been transferred?

We further conduct fine-grained analyses under previous experiment settings trying to answer what knowledge is transferred between structured and

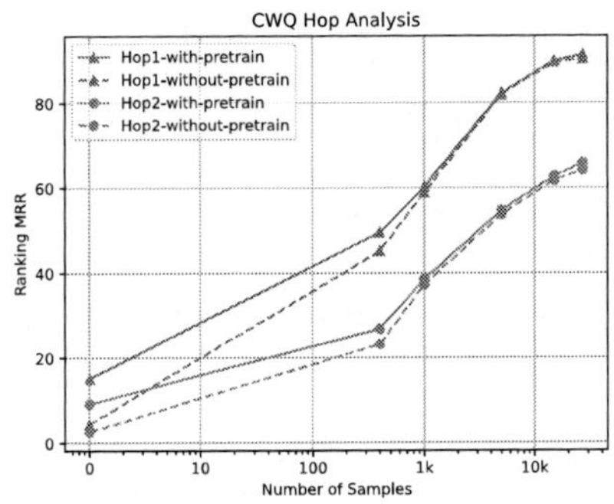

Figure 8: Hop Analysis on the CWQ dataset.

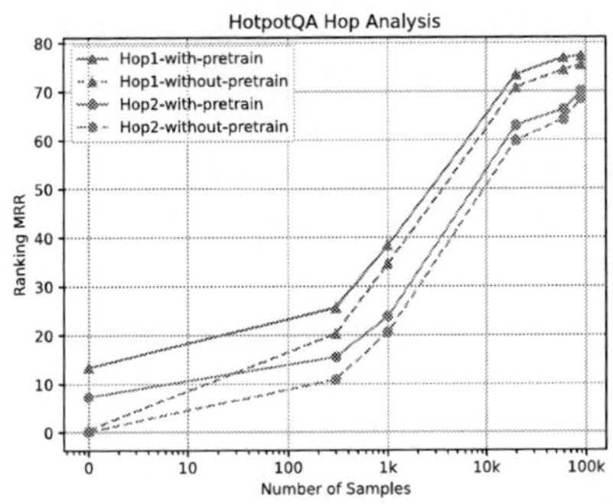

Figure 9: Hop Analysis on the HotpotQA dataset.

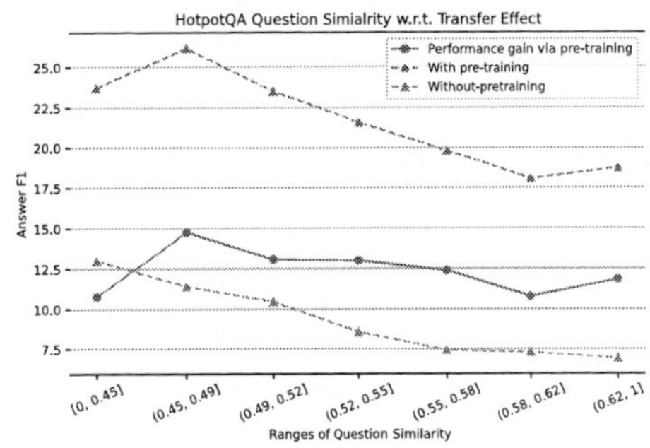

Figure 10: Relationship between question similarity and performance gain.

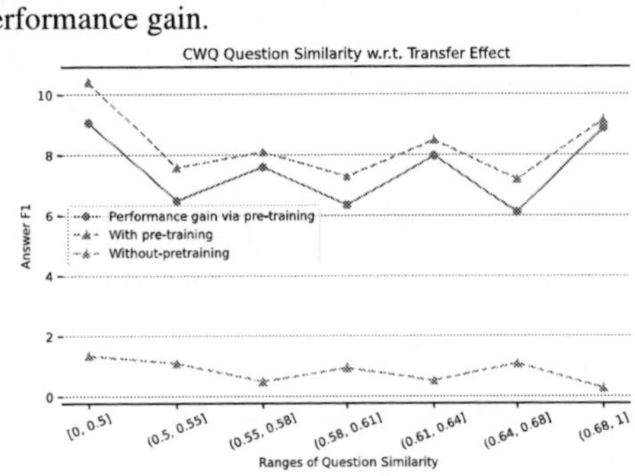

Figure 11: Relationship between question similarity and performance gain on CWQ.

unstructured sources. We hypothesize three major factors that may influence the transfer effect and test their correlations with performance changes.

Reasoning types play a central role in answering complex questions. SIMULTQA is expected to learn similar reasoning processes from structured/unstructured sources if the knowledge about certain reasoning types is transferred. We analyze the transfer effect w.r.t. various reasoning types defined in both datasets (we refer to the original papers (Talmor and Berant, 2018; Yang et al., 2018) for their detailed definitions). As shown in Figure 6 and 7, the most shared two types in both text and KB, composition (i.e., infer the bridge entity) and conjunction (i.e., checking multiple properties) questions are benefited from knowledge transfer the most (especially in the zero-shot transfer), which suggests that SIMULTQA is able to transfer similar reasoning processes between disparate sources regardless of their distinct surface forms.

Another interesting observation is for the Comparison - A/B on HotpotQA (e.g., *Who is older, A or B?*) that has a larger F1 score gain under the zero-shot setting. This type asks a two-choice question which can be answered by locating an entity as the final answer through iteratively retrieving two evidences, which is similar to the chain reasoning in Composition and Conjunction. Although this specific reasoning type is not shared by both sources, the similarity between the reasoning processes makes it benefited from knowledge transfer.

Reasoning hops correspond to decomposed sub-questions from a complex question and we are interested in whether the transfer effect varies according to different hops. In both KBQA and TextQA, the first hop sub-question tends to closely connect with a topic entity or phrase mentioned in the question, while the subsequent (second) hops require more semantic inference to answer the sub-question. As shown in Figure 8, the first hop in CWQ dataset usually gets higher retrieval performance and can be transferred from the other source, which indicates that the knowledge of finding the topic entity in the question is transferred. We also show the hop analysis for HotpotQA in Figure 9. Similar to the observation on CWQ, it shows that the first hop in HotpotQA gets higher retrieval performance and can be transferred from the other source, which further validate that the knowledge of finding the topic entity mentioned in the question is transferred.

Question similarity measures the semantic similarities between questions in testing and training. We hypothesize that the transfer might be easier for testing questions if some similar ones appear in the training. We investigate the zero-shot trans-

Complex question: What is European Union country used the Hungarian forint as its main currency?

Gold KB reasoning path: European Union $\xrightarrow{members}$ y1(CVT) $\xrightarrow{member}$ Hungary $\xleftarrow{currency\_used}$ Forint

Reasoning paths from text source:

1. *(first passage)* The currency of Hungary is the Hungarian forint since 1 August 1946 ...
(second passage) As a member of the European Union, Hungarian government ... replace the forint with the euro.

2. *(first passage)* The forint is the currency of Hungary. ... and the forint has been declared fully convertible.
(second passage) As a member of the European Union, the long-term of aim of the Hungarian government ...

3. *(first passage)* The Gulden or forint was the currency ... and the Austro-Hungarian Monarchy ...
(second passage) In Hungary, the forint was divided into ... for the unit and subunit.

Table 1: Case Study. The question comes from CWQ dataset and is originally answered by a KB reasoning path.

fer to study the influence of pre-training questions more directly. Specifically, for a CWQ question in testing set, we calculate its semantic similarities with all HotpotQA questions in pre-training and take the average of top 5 similarities. We then split CWQ testing questions into several chunks based on this averaged similarity and aggregate their QA performance before and after the pre-training. We do the same thing for the other direction of transfer. We present the relationship between question similarity and performance in HotpotQA on Figure 10. Interestingly, we observe that question similarity is not correlated with transfer effect, i.e., higher similar testing questions are not necessarily to obtain larger performance gain. This finding implies that SIMULTQA transfers the reasoning process in a high-level semantic space rather than through low-level lexical features. We show questions similarity for CWQ in Figure 11, where we also find question similarity is not correlated with the transfer effect.

	Type	%
CWQ	Questions with constraints	50
	Questions with aggregation functions	25
	Others	25
HotpotQA	Relations not covered in KB	45
	Not satisfy chain reasoning	35
	Others	20

Table 2: We manually analyze 20 questions with wrong predicted answers respectively from CWQ and HotpotQA and categorize them.

Error analysis is conducted under the full dataset fine-tuning setting to further understand the transfer behaviors by manually checking errors and categorizing them. As is shown in Table 2, 75% of wrongly answered questions sampled from CWQ contain additional constraints or arithmetic operations which are hard to be supported by text corpus. 45% questions sampled from HotpotQA contain semantic knowledge or relations which cannot be covered in Knowledge Base. 35% of them don't follow the chain reasoning process and are not suitable to be decomposed to answer step by step like KBQA. The other remaining questions are related to errors in retrieval, re-ranking or span extraction process. These unshared knowledge between CWQ and HotpotQA make it reasonable that those wrongly answered questions in one data source cannot be contributed from the other data source.

4.4 RQ3: Answering complex questions by both knowledge sources

To directly measure the transfer effect, in previous sections, the reasoning is always performed on the same knowledge source as where the question is from, e.g., a text-based question is answered by the text reasoning path. Now, we ask whether questions can be better answered by considering both sources. Note that this is a more challenging setting because questions in both datasets only have supervisions from one source, which thus requires stronger transfer signal. Moreover, we can utilize this setting to test how complementary two knowledge sources are, regarding how much they can help each other. Specifically, in addition to the annotated reasoning paths, we collect candidate paths from the other source, i.e., KB paths for text-based questions and text paths for KB-based questions. The final reranking will select the best path from both KB and text paths for all questions. We refer to this setting as the hybrid evaluation.

Our preliminary experiments show that pre-training on one source and then fine-tuning on the other tends to forget the knowledge of the first source, leading to less satisfactory results. Therefore, we jointly train SIMULTQA by iteratively sampling batches from both sources to expose the model to both sources equally in the training time. We then compare the hybrid evaluation with the single-source evaluation in Table 4. For CWQ

(HotpotQA) In the television series Green Hornet, which actor played the role of Kato?
Gold reasoning path from text source: *(first passage)* The Green Hornet is a television series on ABC ... starring Van Williams and Bruce Lee ... *(second passage)* Kato is a fictional character ... was portrayed by Bruce Lee.
Reasoning paths from KB source: 1. Green Hornet $\xleftarrow{series}$ y1(CVT) $\xleftarrow{starring\_roles}$ Bruce Lee $\xleftarrow{actor}$ y2(CVT) $\xleftarrow{appear\_in\_tv\_program}$ Kato 2. Green Hornet $\xleftarrow{film}$ y1(CVT) $\xleftarrow{character}$ Al Hodge $\xleftarrow{notable\_types}$ TV Actor 3. Green Hornet $\xleftarrow{film}$ y1(CVT) $\xleftarrow{character}$ Seth Rogen $\xleftarrow{appeared\_on}$ y2(CVT) $\xleftarrow{appearance\_type}$ Host

Table 3: Case study. The question comes from HotpotQA and is originally answered by a textual reasoning path.

CWQ	F1	Hit@1
SIMULTQA- KB	46.7	47.7
SIMULTQA- Hybrid	48.5	49.8
HotpotQA	**F1**	**EM**
SIMULTQA- Text	71.7	58.8
SIMULTQA- Hybrid	71.2	58.4

Table 4: Comparing single and hybrid evaluations.

dataset, SIMULTQA- Hybrid achieves 1.8 F1 score gains after incorporating text paths for the inference, while the performance of HotpotQA is not influenced in hybrid evaluation after incorporating KB paths. This shows that text knowledge is easier to be transferred to help KB-based questions.

We also conduct case studies by retrieving top-ranked reasoning paths in hybrid evaluation. Table 1 presents a CWQ question and shows that top-ranked text paths are closely related to the golden KB path, indicating that linguistics variants of text knowledge can greatly help KB reasoning. On the other hand, KB knowledge seems to be less helpful to answer text-based questions based on the overall QA performance in Table 4, partially due to the incompatibility between TextQA and KBQA dataset, e.g., entities and relations that cannot be mapped to KB, reasoning types that cannot be answered by KB (see Section 4.3), etc. However, we still find cases in HotpotQA in Table 3 to show KB can somehow contribute to textual reasoning as well.

5 Discussion for future directions

Based on our findings of knowledge transfer for CQA in this paper, we discuss the following directions for future CQA datasets and systems.

Knowledge transfer for efficient CQA dataset annotations. When annotating new CQA datasets whether on text or KB, it would be beneficial to leverage pre-trained SIMULTQA on other sources to discover high-quality reasoning paths for further annotating, which will save much annotation cost.

Diversity of reasoning types. Both text and KB sources are dominant by relatively easy reasoning types, e.g., composition and conjunction. Future CQA datasets should pursue more diverse and harder reasoning types, e.g., types with constraints and arithmetic operations (Dua et al., 2019).

A universal reasoning module. Investigating knowledge transfer between text and KB in this paper suggests that despite the discrepancy of surface forms in different sources, their underlying reasoning processes could be shared. This points out the possibility of learning a universal reasoning process from multiple sources and it is strongly desired to modularize such a reasoning process, which can be injected it into future QA systems.

6 Conclusion

In this paper, we study CQA over structured and unstructured knowledge sources (i.e., KB and text particularly), and focus on studying the knowledge transfer between different knowledge sources. To facilitate the transfer, we first propose a unified CQA framework, SIMULTQA to bridge KBQA and TextQA systems. Empirical results show that knowledge transfer enables substantial improvements on low-resource domains. More importantly, we conduct fine-grained analyses to shed more light on how knowledge is transferred to inspire future research on knowledge transfer between sources, and we conclude the paper with insights for future CQA datasets and systems.

Acknowledgments

The authors would like to thank the reviewers and OSU NLP group members for their thoughtful comments. This research was sponsored in part by Google Faculty Award, NSF IIS-1815674, NSF CAREER #1942980, NSF OAC-2112606.

References

Akari Asai, Kazuma Hashimoto, Hannaneh Hajishirzi, Richard Socher, and Caiming Xiong. 2020. Learning to retrieve reasoning paths over wikipedia graph for question answering. In *International Conference on Learning Representations*.

Junwei Bao, Nan Duan, Zhao Yan, Ming Zhou, and Tiejun Zhao. 2016. Constraint-based question answering with knowledge graph. In *Proceedings of COLING 2016, the 26th International Conference on Computational Linguistics: Technical Papers*, pages 2503–2514.

Jonathan Berant, Andrew Chou, Roy Frostig, and Percy Liang. 2013. Semantic parsing on freebase from question-answer pairs. In *Proceedings of the 2013 Conference on Empirical Methods in Natural Language Processing*, pages 1533–1544.

Danqi Chen, Adam Fisch, Jason Weston, and Antoine Bordes. 2017. Reading wikipedia to answer open-domain questions. In *Proceedings of the 55th Annual Meeting of the Association for Computational Linguistics (Volume 1: Long Papers)*, pages 1870–1879.

Wenhu Chen, Ming-Wei Chang, Eva Schlinger, William Wang, and William W Cohen. 2020a. Open question answering over tables and text. *arXiv preprint arXiv:2010.10439*.

Wenhu Chen, Hanwen Zha, Zhiyu Chen, Wenhan Xiong, Hong Wang, and William Yang Wang. 2020b. Hybridqa: A dataset of multi-hop question answering over tabular and textual data. In *Proceedings of the 2020 Conference on Empirical Methods in Natural Language Processing: Findings*, pages 1026–1036.

Zi-Yuan Chen, Chih-Hung Chang, Yi-Pei Chen, Jijnasa Nayak, and Lun-Wei Ku. 2019. Uhop: An unrestricted-hop relation extraction framework for knowledge-based question answering. In *Proceedings of the 2019 Conference of the North American Chapter of the Association for Computational Linguistics: Human Language Technologies, Volume 1 (Long and Short Papers)*, pages 345–356.

Kevin Clark, Minh-Thang Luong, Urvashi Khandelwal, Christopher D Manning, and Quoc Le. 2019. Bam! born-again multi-task networks for natural language understanding. In *Proceedings of the 57th Annual Meeting of the Association for Computational Linguistics*, pages 5931–5937.

Rajarshi Das, Shehzaad Dhuliawala, Manzil Zaheer, and Andrew McCallum. 2018. Multi-step retriever-reader interaction for scalable open-domain question answering. In *International Conference on Learning Representations*.

Rajarshi Das, Manzil Zaheer, Siva Reddy, and Andrew McCallum. 2017. Question answering on knowledge bases and text using universal schema and memory networks. In *Proceedings of the 55th Annual Meeting of the Association for Computational Linguistics (Volume 2: Short Papers)*, pages 358–365.

Rajarshi Das, Manzil Zaheer, Dung Thai, Ameya Godbole, Ethan Perez, Jay Yoon Lee, Lizhen Tan, Lazaros Polymenakos, and Andrew McCallum. 2021. Case-based reasoning for natural language queries over knowledge bases. In *Proceedings of the 2021 Conference on Empirical Methods in Natural Language Processing*, pages 9594–9611.

Jacob Devlin, Ming-Wei Chang, Kenton Lee, and Kristina Toutanova. 2019. Bert: Pre-training of deep bidirectional transformers for language understanding. In *Proceedings of the 2019 Conference of the North American Chapter of the Association for Computational Linguistics: Human Language Technologies, Volume 1 (Long and Short Papers)*, pages 4171–4186.

Bhuwan Dhingra, Manzil Zaheer, Vidhisha Balachandran, Graham Neubig, Ruslan Salakhutdinov, and William W. Cohen. 2020. Differentiable reasoning over a virtual knowledge base. In *International Conference on Learning Representations*.

Dheeru Dua, Yizhong Wang, Pradeep Dasigi, Gabriel Stanovsky, Sameer Singh, and Matt Gardner. 2019. Drop: A reading comprehension benchmark requiring discrete reasoning over paragraphs. In *Proceedings of NAACL-HLT*, pages 2368–2378.

Yuwei Fang, Siqi Sun, Zhe Gan, Rohit Pillai, Shuohang Wang, and Jingjing Liu. 2020. Hierarchical graph network for multi-hop question answering. In *Proceedings of the 2020 Conference on Empirical Methods in Natural Language Processing (EMNLP)*, pages 8823–8838.

Yair Feldman and Ran El-Yaniv. 2019. Multi-hop paragraph retrieval for open-domain question answering. In *Proceedings of the 57th Annual Meeting of the Association for Computational Linguistics*, pages 2296–2309.

Yu Gu, Sue Kase, Michelle Vanni, Brian Sadler, Percy Liang, Xifeng Yan, and Yu Su. 2020. Beyond iid: Three levels of generalization for question answering on knowledge bases. *arXiv e-prints*, pages arXiv–2011.

Vladimir Karpukhin, Barlas Oguz, Sewon Min, Patrick Lewis, Ledell Wu, Sergey Edunov, Danqi Chen, and Wen-tau Yih. 2020. Dense passage retrieval for open-domain question answering. In *Proceedings of the 2020 Conference on Empirical Methods in Natural Language Processing (EMNLP)*, pages 6769–6781.

Yunshi Lan and Jing Jiang. 2020. Query graph generation for answering multi-hop complex questions from knowledge bases. In *Proceedings of the 58th Annual Meeting of the Association for Computational Linguistics*, pages 969–974.

Yunshi Lan, Shuohang Wang, and Jing Jiang. 2019. Multi-hop knowledge base question answering with an iterative sequence matching model. In *2019 IEEE International Conference on Data Mining (ICDM)*, pages 359–368. IEEE.

Jinhyuk Lee, Seongjun Yun, Hyunjae Kim, Miyoung Ko, and Jaewoo Kang. 2018. Ranking paragraphs for improving answer recall in open-domain question answering. In *Proceedings of the 2018 Conference on Empirical Methods in Natural Language Processing*, pages 565–569.

Xiaodong Liu, Pengcheng He, Weizhu Chen, and Jianfeng Gao. 2019. Multi-task deep neural networks for natural language understanding. In *Proceedings of the 57th Annual Meeting of the Association for Computational Linguistics*, pages 4487–4496.

Kangqi Luo, Fengli Lin, Xusheng Luo, and Kenny Zhu. 2018. Knowledge base question answering via encoding of complex query graphs. In *Proceedings of the 2018 Conference on Empirical Methods in Natural Language Processing*, pages 2185–2194.

Gaurav Maheshwari, Priyansh Trivedi, Denis Lukovnikov, Nilesh Chakraborty, Asja Fischer, and Jens Lehmann. 2019. Learning to rank query graphs for complex question answering over knowledge graphs. In *International semantic web conference*, pages 487–504. Springer.

Todor Mihaylov and Anette Frank. 2018. Knowledgeable reader: Enhancing cloze-style reading comprehension with external commonsense knowledge. In *Proceedings of the 56th Annual Meeting of the Association for Computational Linguistics (Volume 1: Long Papers)*, pages 821–832.

Sewon Min, Danqi Chen, Luke Zettlemoyer, and Hannaneh Hajishirzi. 2019. Knowledge guided text retrieval and reading for open domain question answering. *arXiv preprint arXiv:1911.03868*.

Yixin Nie, Songhe Wang, and Mohit Bansal. 2019. Revealing the importance of semantic retrieval for machine reading at scale. In *Proceedings of the 2019 Conference on Empirical Methods in Natural Language Processing and the 9th International Joint Conference on Natural Language Processing (EMNLP-IJCNLP)*, pages 2553–2566.

Barlas Oguz, Xilun Chen, Vladimir Karpukhin, Stan Peshterliev, Dmytro Okhonko, Michael Schlichtkrull, Sonal Gupta, Yashar Mehdad, and Scott Yih. 2020. Unified open-domain question answering with structured and unstructured knowledge. *arXiv preprint arXiv:2012.14610*.

Sinno Jialin Pan and Qiang Yang. 2009. A survey on transfer learning. *IEEE Transactions on knowledge and data engineering*, 22(10):1345–1359.

Matthew Peters, Mark Neumann, Mohit Iyyer, Matt Gardner, Christopher Clark, Kenton Lee, and Luke Zettlemoyer. 2018. Deep contextualized word representations. In *Proceedings of the 2018 Conference of the North American Chapter of the Association for Computational Linguistics: Human Language Technologies, Volume 1 (Long Papers)*, pages 2227–2237.

Peng Qi, Haejun Lee, Oghenetegiri Sido, Christopher D Manning, et al. 2020. Retrieve, rerank, read, then iterate: Answering open-domain questions of arbitrary complexity from text. *arXiv preprint arXiv:2010.12527*.

Peng Qi, Xiaowen Lin, Leo Mehr, Zijian Wang, and Christopher D Manning. 2019. Answering complex open-domain questions through iterative query generation. In *Proceedings of the 2019 Conference on Empirical Methods in Natural Language Processing and the 9th International Joint Conference on Natural Language Processing (EMNLP-IJCNLP)*, pages 2590–2602.

Alec Radford, Karthik Narasimhan, Tim Salimans, and Ilya Sutskever. 2018. Improving language understanding by generative pre-training (2018).

Colin Raffel, Noam Shazeer, Adam Roberts, Katherine Lee, Sharan Narang, Michael Matena, Yanqi Zhou, Wei Li, and Peter J Liu. 2020. Exploring the limits of transfer learning with a unified text-to-text transformer. *Journal of Machine Learning Research*, 21(140):1–67.

Pranav Rajpurkar, Jian Zhang, Konstantin Lopyrev, and Percy Liang. 2016. Squad: 100,000+ questions for machine comprehension of text. In *Proceedings of the 2016 Conference on Empirical Methods in Natural Language Processing*, pages 2383–2392.

Sebastian Ruder, Matthew E Peters, Swabha Swayamdipta, and Thomas Wolf. 2019. Transfer learning in natural language processing. In *Proceedings of the 2019 conference of the North American chapter of the association for computational linguistics: Tutorials*, pages 15–18.

Jiaxin Shi, Shulin Cao, Lei Hou, Juanzi Li, and Hanwang Zhang. 2021. Transfernet: An effective and transparent framework for multi-hop question answering over relation graph. In *Proceedings of the 2021 Conference on Empirical Methods in Natural Language Processing*, pages 4149–4158.

Haitian Sun, Tania Bedrax-Weiss, and William Cohen. 2019. Pullnet: Open domain question answering with iterative retrieval on knowledge bases and text. In *Proceedings of the 2019 Conference on Empirical Methods in Natural Language Processing and the 9th International Joint Conference on Natural Language Processing (EMNLP-IJCNLP)*, pages 2380–2390.

Haitian Sun, Bhuwan Dhingra, Manzil Zaheer, Kathryn Mazaitis, Ruslan Salakhutdinov, and William Cohen. 2018. Open domain question answering using early fusion of knowledge bases and text. In *Proceedings of the 2018 Conference on Empirical Methods in Natural Language Processing*, pages 4231–4242.

Alon Talmor and Jonathan Berant. 2018. The web as a knowledge-base for answering complex questions. In *Proceedings of the 2018 Conference of the North*

American Chapter of the Association for Computational Linguistics: Human Language Technologies, Volume 1 (Long Papers), pages 641–651.

Shuohang Wang, Mo Yu, Xiaoxiao Guo, Zhiguo Wang, Tim Klinger, Wei Zhang, Shiyu Chang, Gerald Tesauro, Bowen Zhou, and Jing Jiang. 2018. R3: Reinforced ranker-reader for open-domain question answering.

Wenhan Xiong, Xiang Li, Srini Iyer, Jingfei Du, Patrick Lewis, William Yang Wang, Yashar Mehdad, Scott Yih, Sebastian Riedel, Douwe Kiela, and Barlas Oguz. 2021. Answering complex open-domain questions with multi-hop dense retrieval. In *International Conference on Learning Representations*.

Wenhan Xiong, Mo Yu, Shiyu Chang, Xiaoxiao Guo, and William Yang Wang. 2019. Improving question answering over incomplete kbs with knowledge-aware reader. In *Proceedings of the 57th Annual Meeting of the Association for Computational Linguistics*, pages 4258–4264.

Wei Yang, Yuqing Xie, Aileen Lin, Xingyu Li, Luchen Tan, Kun Xiong, Ming Li, and Jimmy Lin. 2019. End-to-end open-domain question answering with bertserini. In *Proceedings of the 2019 Conference of the North American Chapter of the Association for Computational Linguistics (Demonstrations)*, pages 72–77.

Zhilin Yang, Peng Qi, Saizheng Zhang, Yoshua Bengio, William Cohen, Ruslan Salakhutdinov, and Christopher D Manning. 2018. Hotpotqa: A dataset for diverse, explainable multi-hop question answering. In *Proceedings of the 2018 Conference on Empirical Methods in Natural Language Processing*, pages 2369–2380.

Xi Ye, Semih Yavuz, Kazuma Hashimoto, Yingbo Zhou, and Caiming Xiong. 2021. Rng-kbqa: Generation augmented iterative ranking for knowledge base question answering. In *Proceedings of the Annual Meeting of the Association for Computational Linguistics (ACL)*.

Wen-tau Yih, Ming-Wei Chang, Xiaodong He, and Jianfeng Gao. 2015. Semantic parsing via staged query graph generation: Question answering with knowledge base. In *Proceedings of the 53rd Annual Meeting of the Association for Computational Linguistics and the 7th International Joint Conference on Natural Language Processing (Volume 1: Long Papers)*, pages 1321–1331.

Yunchang Zhu, Liang Pang, Yanyan Lan, Huawei Shen, and Xueqi Cheng. 2021. Adaptive information seeking for open-domain question answering. In *Proceedings of the 2021 Conference on Empirical Methods in Natural Language Processing*, pages 3615–3626.

Hierarchical Control of Situated Agents through Natural Language

Shuyan Zhou, Pengcheng Yin, Graham Neubig
Language Technologies Institute
Carnegie Mellon University
{shuyanzh, pcyin, gneubig}@cs.cmu.edu

Abstract

When humans perform a particular task, they do so hierarchically: splitting higher-level tasks into smaller sub-tasks. However, most works on natural language (NL) command of situated agents have treated the procedures to be executed as flat sequences of simple actions, or any hierarchies of procedures have been shallow at best. In this paper, we propose a formalism of *procedures as programs*, a method for representing hierarchical procedural knowledge for agent command and control aimed at enabling easy application to various scenarios. We further propose a modeling paradigm of *hierarchical modular networks*, which consist of a *planner* and *reactors* that convert NL intents to predictions of executable programs and probe the environment for information necessary to complete the program execution. We instantiate this framework on the IQA and ALFRED datasets for NL instruction following. Our model outperforms reactive baselines by a large margin on both datasets. We also demonstrate that our framework is more data-efficient, and that it allows for fast iterative development.[1]

1 Introduction

Procedural knowledge, or "how-to" knowledge, refers to knowledge of how to execute particular tasks. It is inherently hierarchical; high-level procedures consist of many lower-level procedures. For example, "cooking a pizza" comprises many lower-level procedures, including "buying ingredients", "knead dough", etc. There are also multiple levels of hierarchy; "buying ingredients" can be further decomposed to "go to a grocery", "paying" etc.

There has been significant prior work on benchmarks and methods for complex task completion using situated agents given natural language (NL) instructions, such as agents trained to navigate the web and mobile UIs (Li et al., 2020; Xu et al., 2021) or solve household tasks (Shridhar et al., 2020a). However, most methods applied to these tasks use a *reactive* strategy that makes decisions on the low-level atomic actions available to the agent while making steps through the environment (Gupta et al., 2017; Zhu et al., 2020), or define procedures in a shallow way where there only exists one level of hierarchy (Andreas et al., 2017; Gordon et al., 2018; Yu et al., 2019; Das et al., 2019).These approaches are often data-inefficient due to the semantic gap between abstract natural language instructions and concrete executions. In contrast, several works have demonstrated that using specially designed intermediate representations tailored to individual tasks (Chen and Mooney, 2011; Artzi and Zettlemoyer, 2013; Misra et al., 2016) can help reduce this expense and improve performance, albeit at the cost of significant effort on the part of the researchers devising these methods.

In this paper, we propose a framework to improve the execution of complex natural language commands (example in Fig. 1) by expressing *procedures as programs* (PaP) written in a high-level programming language like Python (§4). This makes it easy for human engineers to *express and leverage their hierarchical procedural knowledge*, and the execution of each program yields actions to accomplish a task described in NL. There are several merits to this approach. First, programs are inherently hierarchical; they apply nested function calls to realize higher-level functionality with multiple calls to lower-level functionality. Second, programs have built-in control-flow operators, making it possible to deal with multiple divergent situations without the loss of higher-level abstraction. Third, programs provide a flexible way to define, share and call different machine-learned components to perceive the environment through an embodied agent's executions. Finally, programs in a familiar high-level programming language are comprehensible and curatable, allowing for fast development on

[1] All code will be released upon acceptance.

Proceedings of the Workshop on Structured and Unstructured Knowledge Integration (SUKI), pages 67 - 84
July 14, 2022 ©2022 Association for Computational Linguistics

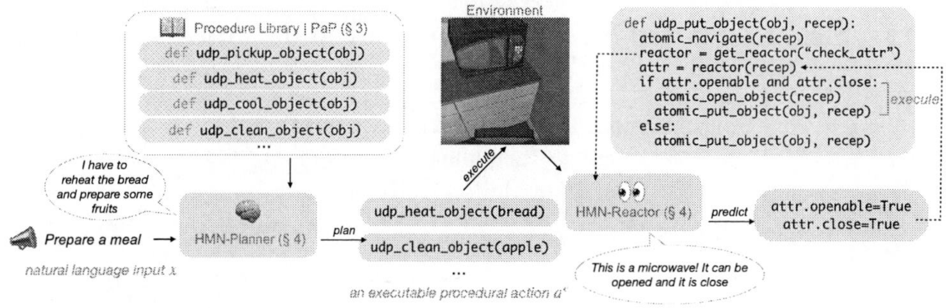

Figure 1: The proposed framework, containing a hierarchical library of procedures written as Python functions (§4). Coupled with this library is a hierarchical neural network (HMN, §5) with a PLANNER that constructs an executable procedure and REACTORS that react to the environment to resolve control flow.

various tasks. These four features remain largely unexplored in the existing representations (Chen and Mooney, 2011; Artzi and Zettlemoyer, 2013; Misra et al., 2016), as discussed further in §2.

Coupled with this representation, we propose a modeling paradigm of *hierarchical modular networks* (HMN; §5) that has (1) a learnable PLANNER that maps NL to the corresponding executable programs and (2) a collection of REACTORS that perceive the environment and provide context-sensitive feedback to decide the further execution of the program. Such modular design can facilitate training efficiency and improve the performance of each individual component (Andreas et al., 2016).

We instantiate our framework on two task settings: the IQA dataset (Gordon et al., 2018) where an agent explores the environment to answer questions regarding objects; and the ALFRED dataset (Shridhar et al., 2020a), in which an agent must map natural language instructions to actions to complete household tasks (§6). In experiments (§7), we find that our framework outperforms the reactive baseline by a significant margin on both datasets, and is significantly more data-efficient. We also demonstrate the flexibility of our framework for fast iterative development of program libraries. We end with a discussion of the limitations of the framework and the potential solutions, paving the way for future works that scale our framework to more open-domain tasks (§7).

2 Contrast to Previous Formalisms

While designing intermediate representations that stand between NL and low-level actions *for individual tasks* has been studied in the literature, our goal is to design a framework that makes it simple to design such representations *for new tasks*, with a particular focus on capturing the hierarchical nature of procedures. In contrast to most previous works in this area, which employ relatively esoteric representation methods such as lambda calculus (Artzi and Zettlemoyer, 2013; Artzi et al., 2014), PaP uses widely-adopted general-purpose programming languages (*e.g.* Python) to specify and represent hierarchical procedures. These are comprehensible to most engineers and do not require system designers to learn a new task-specific language. PaP also enable easy creation of more hierarchical procedures with *reusable sub-routines*. Existing works either do not model such sub-procedures as reusable components (Misra et al., 2016), or define procedures as a flat sequence of actions without any hierarchy (Chen et al., 2020; Artzi and Zettlemoyer, 2013). The hierarchical procedures with reusable sub-routines is also reminiscent of works in semantic parsing, which compose programs from idiomatic program structures (Iyer et al., 2017; Shin et al., 2019). More discussions are in §E.

Additionally, PaP uses control flow with divergent branches to handle environment-specific variations of a high-level procedure. A single procedure could therefore dynamically adapt to a variety of environments following the branches triggered by the environments. This makes our representations more compact. This feature also allows developers to easily inject human priors of executions traces under different conditions, which might be challenging to learn in a data-efficient manner. To our best knowledge, this feature is largely unexplored in the literature on designing intermediate representations for agent control.

Finally, PaP provides a convenient interface for procedures to query and interact with task-specific situated components (*e.g.* a visual component). Under PaP, situated components are exposed as predefined APIs, and can be easily called by high-level procedures. In contrast, existing works either require separate mechanisms to call such components (Misra et al., 2016), or the environment where they are expected to work is less complex, and thus the flexible use of a collection of situated components is not a necessity (Chen and Mooney, 2011).

We can also view the PaP formalism as a way to construct behavior trees (Colledanchise and Ögren, 2018), which have been used in robotic planning and game design literature. We can use the off-the-shelf tools to convert the programs to abstract syntax trees (AST) which resemble these trees. Previous works on robotics also leverage planning domain definition language (PDDL) and answer set planners (ASP) for task planning (Jiang et al., 2019b), which is conceptually different from our formalism. PDDL+ASP searches for an action sequences based on the initial and the final states, while our formalism focuses on describing the actual procedure used to accomplish a task.

3 Task: Controlling Situated Agents

First, we define the task of controlling an agent in some situated environment $\mathcal{E}$ through natural language. The environment $\mathcal{E}$ provides a set of atomic actions $\mathcal{A}^a = \{a_1^a, a_2^a, ...\}$ to interact with the environment. Each atomic action can take zero or more arguments that specify which parts of the environment to which it is to be applied. We denote action a_i^a's jth argument as $r_{i,j}$. The specific type of each argument will depend on the action and environment; it could be discrete symbols, scalar values, tensors describing regions of the visual space, etc. Given a user intent $\boldsymbol{x}$, the control system aims at creating an atomic action sequence consisting of a sequence of actions $\boldsymbol{a} = [a_1, a_2, ...]$ ($a_i \in \mathcal{A}^a$) and concrete assignments $\boldsymbol{r}$ for each of these n actions. This action sequence is executed against the environment to achieve a result $\hat{y} = \mathcal{E}(\boldsymbol{a}, \boldsymbol{r})$, which is compared against a gold-standard result y using a score function $s(y, \hat{y})$. Action sequences realizing the intent will receive a high score, and those that do not will receive a low score.

4 Representing Procedures as Programs

Next, we introduce the main components of our formalism. A few examples are listed in Tab. 1.[2]

[2]Since actions are implemented as functions, we use "action" and "function" interchangeably.

```
# C1: an atomic action to toggle on an appliance
def atomic_toggle_on(obj):
    env.call("toggle_on", obj)
# C2: a procedural action to pick and then put an object
def udp_pick_and_put_object(obj, dst):
    udp_pickup_object(obj)
    udp_put_object(obj, dst)
# C3: an emptying receptacle procedure with for-loop
def udp_empty_recep(recep, dst):
    reactor = get_reactor("find_all_obj")
    obj_list = reactor(recep)
    for obj in obj_list:
        udp_pick_and_put_object(obj, dst)
# C4: a pickup object procedure with control flow
def udp_pickup_object(obj):
    atomic_navigate(obj)
    reactor1 = get_reactor("find_recep")
    reactor2 = get_reactor("check_obj_attr")
    recep = reactor1(obj)
    attr = reactor2(recep)
    if attr.openable and attr.close:
        atomic_open_object(recep)
        atomic_pickup_object(obj)
        atomic_close_object(recep)
    else: atomic_pickup_object(obj)
```

Table 1: Atomic and procedural action functions in Python, starting with `atomic` and udp respectively.

Interface to Atomic Actions $\mathcal{A}^a$ (C1) Atomic actions provide a medium for direct interaction with the environment. The call of an atomic action with proper argument types will invoke the corresponding execution in the environment.

Procedural Actions $\mathcal{A}^p$ (C2-C4) Procedural actions describe abstractions of higher-level procedures composed of either lower-level procedures or atomic actions. Notably, lower-level procedures can be *re-used* across many higher-level procedures without re-definition. Formalizing the hierarchies in this compact way can not only facilitate the procedure library curation process but also potentially benefit automatic library induction (e.g. through minimal description length (Ellis et al., 2020)).

Control-flow of $\mathcal{A}^p$ (C3-C4) There can be multiple execution traces to accomplish the same goal under different conditions. For example, picking up an object from inside a closed receptacle requires opening the receptacle first, while the open action is not required for objects not in a receptacle. To improve the *coverage* of procedural functions we leverage the built-in control flow of the host programming language to allow for conditional execution of environment-specific actions (**C4**). To deal with the repeated calls of the same routine, we further introduce for/while-loops. For example, **C3** works for emptying receptacles with variable number of objects without repeatedly writing down the `udp_pick_put_object`. Leveraging control flows to describe divergent procedural traces remains largely unexplored in previous works.

Call of Situated Components (C3-C4) The dynamic trigger of a control flow often remain unknown before the agent interacts with the environment. We introduce situated components to probe the environment and gather state information to guide program execution. In **C4**, the agent uses two different reactors to find the potential holder of an object (`reactor1`) and exam the holder's properties (`reactor2`). A reactor can be implemented in many ways (*e.g.* using a neural network).

5 Hierarchical Modular Networks

This section introduces how to use the procedure library $\mathcal{A}$ to generate executable programs to complete tasks described in natural language x. We propose a modeling method of *hierarchical modular networks* (HMN) that consists of two main components. First, there is a HMN-PLANNER that convert x to an executable procedural action $a^e = \{a_1, a_2, ..., a_n\}$ where a_i either belongs to atomic functions $\mathcal{A}^a$ or procedural functions $\mathcal{A}^p$. We model the HMN-PLANNER as a sequence-to-sequence model where the encoder takes x as input, and the decoder generates one function a_i at a time from a constrained vocabulary $\mathcal{A}^p \bigcup \mathcal{A}^a$, conditioned on x and the action history $\{a_1, ..., a_{i-1}\}$.

Next, we define the collection of situated components, "reactors," as HMN-REACTORS. Each reactor is a classifier that predicts one or many labels given the observed information (*e.g.* the NL input, the visual observation. For example, `reactor2` in **C4** in Tab. 1 probes the status of a receptacle based on receptacle name and the visual input. HMN-REACTORS allows us to flexibly share the same reactor among different functions and design separated reactors to serve different purposes. For example in **C4**, we use two reactors to find the possible receptacle of an object (`reactor1`) and to perceive the open/closed status of a receptacle (`reactor2`) since these two tasks presumably require more mutually exclusive information. At the same time, we share `reactor2` to also probe the related `openable` property of a receptacle for more efficient parameter sharing. This sort of modular design leads to efficient training and improved performance (Andreas et al., 2016).

6 Instantiations

In this section, we introduce two concrete realizations of the proposed framework over the IQA dataset (Gordon et al., 2018) and the ALFRED dataset (Shridhar et al., 2020a). Both are based on egocentric vision in a high-fidelity simulated environment THOR (Deitke et al., 2020).

6.1 IQA

IQA is a dataset for situated question answering with three types of questions querying (1) the existence of an object (*e.g. Is there a mug?*), (2) the count of an object (*e.g. How many mugs are there?*) and (3) whether a receptacle contains an object (*e.g. Is there a mug in the fridge?*).

There are seven atomic actions in IQA, *i.e.* `Moveahead`, `RotateLeft`, `RotateRight`, `LookDown`, `LookUp`, `Open` and `Close`; and all arguments are expressed through the unique object IDs (*e.g.* `apple_1`). We further process the atomic navigation actions to a single atomic action `Navigate` with one argument `destination`, which moves the agent directly to the destination. This replacement is done by searching the scene and recording the coordinates of unmovable objects (*e.g.* cabinet) – more details provided in the §C.1.

Procedure Library We design a procedure for each of the three types of questions in IQA, as shown in Tab. 2. Generally speaking, those procedures first search all or a subset of the receptacles (*e.g.*`table`, `fridge`) in a scene for the target object (*e.g.*mug), and then execute a question-specific intent (*e.g.* existence-checking, counting). Tab. 2 shows the procedure for answering existence questions. Since the target object can be inside a receptacle (*e.g.* fridge), we introduce control flow to decide whether to open and close a receptacle before and after checking its contents in sub-procedure `udp_check_relation`. Following the paper author's understanding of the three types of questions, these procedural functions were created without looking into any actual trajectories that answer these questions. In total, we define six procedural actions with a complete list in §A.

HMN The natural language questions x in IQA are generated with a limited number of templates. There are only seven receptacles, and three of them are openable. We thus use a rule-based HMN-PLANNER to map a template to one of the three high-level procedural actions (*i.e.* existence, count and contain). Then, we design two reactors, each as a multi-classes classifier: ATTRCHECKER, which examines the properties (whether the object is openable) and the status (whether the object is opened) of an object, and RELCHECKER, which checks the spatial relation between two objects. We leave the

```
# check existence of an object in the scene
def udp_check_obj_exist(obj):
    all_recep = udp_grid_search_recep()
    for recep in all_recep:
        rel = udp_check_relation(obj, recep)
        if rel == OBJ_IN_RECEP:
            return True
    return False
# check object inside receptacle
def udp_check_relation(obj, recep):
    atomic_navigate(recep)
    r1 = get_reactor("check_obj_attr")
    r2 = get_reactor("check_obj_recep_rel")
    attr = r1(recep)
    if attr.is_openable and attr.is_closed:
        atomic_open_object(recep)
        rel = r2(obj, recep)
        atomic_close_object(recep)
    else:
        rel = r2(obj, recep)
    return rel
```

Table 2: The procedural actions to answer the existence questions of the IQA dataset.

detailed implementations of the reactors to §C.3. Notably, we use *zero* IQA training data to build the HMN. Instead, it is made up of a few heuristic components based on the predictions of a pre-trained perception component.

6.2 ALFRED

ALFRED is a benchmark for mapping NL instructions to actions to accomplish household tasks in the situated environment (*e.g.* heat an egg). Examples in ALFRED come with both single-sentence high-level intents describing a goal (*e.g.* the NL input in Fig. 1), and more fine-grained, step-by-step instructions. In this paper we only use the high-level intents, a more realistic yet more challenging setting to study the effectiveness of our framework in encoding extra procedural knowledge for under-specified intents. Besides the seven atomic actions in the IQA dataset, ALFRED also introduces `Pickup`, `Put`, `ToggleOn`, `ToggleOff` for object interactions. ALFRED uses 2D binary tensor describing regions of the visual space as arguments. Similarly to IQA, we replace the navigation action with an atomic action `Navigate destination`. Previous works also apply similar replacement (Shridhar et al., 2020b; Karamcheti et al., 2020) to allow the agent to proceed to a location without fail. Details in §C.

Procedure Library We create a procedure library for ALFRED by identifying idiomatic control flow and operations from a small set of randomly sampled examples. The library is designed with two goals in mind as discussed in §4: *reusability*, where a single function can be applied to multiple similar scenarios, and *coverage*, where a function should cover different execution trajectories under different conditions For instance, many tasks consist of a sub-routine to obtain an object by first navigating to the object and then picking up the object by hand, calling for a reusable procedure adaptable to those scenarios. Moreover, if an object is positioned inside a receptacle, picking up the object would require opening the receptacle first, an edge case that should be covered by relevant procedures (*e.g.* **C4** in Tab. 1). Notably, we constrain the conditions of the control flow to the logic operation of the property values of objects (*e.g.* `fridge.is_openable=True`).

In total, we define ten such procedural actions (complete list in §A). This creation process was done by the first author, a graduate student proficient in Python, and took about two hours. This modest amount of time is partially due to PaP's intuitive interface that allows for quick summarization of complex procedures and partially due to ALFRED's relative simplicity; it has a limited number of task types and consistent execution traces. A sanity check of an initial version of the library uncovered some mismatches (details in §C.4). For example, a laptop should be closed before picking up, which was not captured by our library. We thus added a `udp_close_if_needed` function call before the `atomic_pick_object` in `udp_pick_object`. On one hand this increases the complexity of the library design process, but on the other hand it also demonstrates the flexibility of the PaP framework, as the necessary fixes could be done entirely by modifying the procedure library itself. §7.1 provides an end-to-end comparison with different procedural libraries.

To investigate the scalability of our annotation process, we also provided a similar guideline and the 21 examples to a separate programmer who does not have any prior knowledge to the dataset. We found that the programmer could quickly understand the PaP Python interface and issue reasonable procedural functions that highly resemble our own creations. This indicates the possibility to curate the procedure libraries with crowd-sourcing efforts. More discussion is provided in §7.2 and the full list of the annotation guideline and the user-issued functions are listed in §B.

HMN As discussed in §5, HMN-PLANNER generates an executable procedural action $\boldsymbol{a}^e$, given the natural language instruction $\boldsymbol{x}$. We implement our planner with a sequence-to-sequence model with

```
# C1, heat an object with microwave
def udp_heat_object(obj):
    udp_pick_and_put_object(obj, microwave)
    atomic_toggleon_object(microwave)
    atomic_toggleoff_object(microwave)
# C2, prepare the receptacle for future interactions
def udp_prepare_recep(obj):
    reactor = get_reactor("check_obj_attr")
    attr = reactor(obj)
    if attr.is_openable and attr.is_closed:
        atomic_open_object(obj)
```

Table 3: Two procedural actions for ALFRED

attention (Bahdanau et al., 2015).

Based on the construction of the procedure library and the required argument type, we design three reactors: ATTRCHECKER, which has the same functionality as in IQA, REFINDER, which probes where the desired object lies by predicting a receptacle name from all available receptacles to the dataset, and MGENERATOR, which generates the 2D binary tensor representing the interaction region. Since ALFRED has much richer scene configurations and more diverse objects than IQA, the reactors are fully implemented with neural networks.This demonstrates the flexibility of our framework to share, add and replace components to suit different situations. We describe the detailed implementations of the reactors in §C.3. The HMN is trained in a supervised fashion, and the heuristic way to induce the supervisions from the original dataset is described in §C.4.

7 Experiments

We compare our proposed framework with the baseline reactive agents that predicts a single atomic action at each time step. Notably, we apply the same pretrained vision models, pre-searched map and the `Navigate` atomic action used in PaP-HMN to the baseline to ensure a fair comparison. More details in §C.2. We attempt to answer the following research questions: (1) Does our framework performs better in complex tasks with inherent hierarchical structures, comparing to a purely reactive system? If so, in what way? (2) Can our framework leverage the procedural knowledge encoded in the procedure library and the modularity of its HMN to learn more efficiently? And (3) Can our framework accelerate the development of the task of interest?

7.1 Results on IQA

Results in Tab. 6 show that our framework yields the best performance across all models over different question types. Through error analysis, we

[3] *unseen* features the out-of-distribution visual appearances and arrangements of objects, same for ALFRED

		EX	CNT	CT
A3C	*seen*	-	-	-
	unseen	48.6	24.5	49.9
HIMN	*seen*	73.7	36.3	60.7
	unseen	68.5	30.4	58.7
Reactive	*seen*	50.0	25.1	49.6
	unseen	18.9	9.1	30.6
PaP-HMN	*seen*	**82.8**	**43.8**	**82.2**
	unseen	**83.8**	**45.2**	**83.1**
PaP$_{v0.1}$-HMN	*seen*	80.3	41.5	75.7

Table 4: The answer accuracy (%) over IQA dataset on existence (EX), counting (CNT) and contain (CT) questions. The results of AC3 and HIMN are from Gordon et al. (2018). **Bold** shows the best performance[3]

observe that while the reactive model can generate reasonable action sequences *seen*, its answers are no better than a random guess. This indicates the inability of a reactive model to book-keep the observed objects in the memory. For *unseen*, we find that the baseline model skips predicting some receptacles or even generates syntactically invalid sequences (*e.g.* functions without required arguments). This is surprising, since the reactive baseline is trained using the *canonicalized* action sequences according to the roll-out of the for-loops in the procedure library, which are quite regular. This indicates that even simple repeated procedures can be easily represented with a for/while-loop can still be challenging to a reactive agent implemented with a sequence-based backbone. The strong performance of PaP might seem unsurprising given that the library is tailored carefully to the domain. However, sophisticated models like HIMN (Gordon et al., 2018) still struggle to capture such simple patterns, and there is not a straightforward way to plug the simple rules that we were easily able to describe in PaP in to improve its performance; PaP solves the easy problems so that an ML model can focus its effort on the more challenging problems that truly require learning (*e.g.* object grounding).

Procedure Library Manipulation One advantage of our approach is that it decouples the reactors from the creation of the procedural knowledge, thus allowing plug-in update of the procedure library without time-consuming redesigning or retraining the reactors. Tab. 5 lists two versions of the procedure that decides the list of receptacles to enumerate, and the results of v0.1 are shown at the bottom of Tab. 4. In v0.1, the agent stands in its randomly initialized position, looks around, and detects receptacles. Only the detected recepta-

```
# v0.1: only scan at the start position
def udp_search_recep():
    r = get_reactor("detect_recep")
    receps = []
    for rotation in range(0, 360, 90):
        atomic_rotate(rotation)
        for horizon in [-30, 0, 30]:
            atomic_look(horizon)
            receps += r()
    return receps
# now: navigate to every reachable point and scan
def udp_grid_search_recep():
    if not done_search:
        all_receps = [] # global var
        for pos in reachable_pos:
            atomic_navigate_pos(pos)
            all_receps += udp_search_recep()
    return all_receps
```

Table 5: Two versions for getting receptacles.

	seen	*unseen*
Singh et al. (2020)	5.4	0.2
Reactive	21.0	5.6
PaP-HMN	**27.0**	**11.7**
Reactive + Oracle MG	40.7 (48.6)	36.4 (45.0)
PaP-HMN + Oracle MG	**54.5 (61.0)**	**51.3 (61.1)**

Table 6: The full task success rate SR (the partial task success rate, SSR, %) of the baseline reactive model and our model. MG represents the mask generator. **bold** shows the best performance for each setting.

cles are checked to answer the question. However, since not all receptacles are visible to the agent at the agent's initial point, such checking could be incomplete. We upgraded this function to the new version where the agent searches all possible positions of the scene and memorizes the unmovable receptacle positions. This process only happens once for a scene, and the searched map is stored for future uses. In this way, most receptacles are covered. This simple modification without changing the remaining parts of the framework improved the CT answer accuracy by 6.6% and improvement of around 2.5% over the other two question types.

7.2 Results on ALFRED

Tab. 6 lists the results. Our model yields a consistent gain over the baseline system on both splits.[4] In our analysis, we find that the Mask R-CNN vision model is the main bottleneck of both end-to-end systems, which we hypothesis is due to the sub-optimal transfer from the MSCOCO (Lin et al., 2014) to the ALFRED data. It frequently misclassifies the object types or does not recognize the object in the scene at all. This results in the failure of object grounding and thus the failure of the task completion. Since the development of a better object detector is somewhat orthogonal to our main contributions, to isolate the impact of using a weak object detector on the end-to-end performance, we replace the Mask R-CNN with an oracle object mask generator, which always localize and interact with the provided object name if the object is in view for all experiments below. We observe a larger performance gap using this oracle mask generator as shown in the bottom half of Tab. 6. This gap suggests that procedural knowledge that could be summarized as several functions describable within a short period of time (in this case, ten functions in two hours) can still be difficult for a reactive system to capture. While the same procedural knowledge can be used in many cases with different environment dynamics, a reactive system struggle to distill such knowledge when interacting with highly diverse and dynamic environments.

Performance w.r.t. Action Length In Fig. 2, we further break down the results to buckets w.r.t the length of atomic action sequences (without arguments), which roughly represents the difficulty of a task. We observe consistent improvements over all buckets, This difference is even more obvious for challenging tasks with over 21 atomic actions. Our model maintains similar performance for such cases on *seen*, and being able to accomplish 30% tasks successfully on *unseen*, while the baseline can barely complete any task. These suggest our framework's stronger capacity to solve long-horizon tasks of deeper hierarchies.

Data Efficiency The hierarchical procedural knowledge could potentially allow the system to learn task completion in a data-efficient manner. We benchmark HMN with varying amounts of training data. As shown in Fig. 2, with 20% of the training data, our method exceeds the baseline with the full training set by a large margin (7.7% and 17.3% respectively). Furthermore, for *seen*, the baseline only obtains less than 60% SR with 20% training data, compared to the full data; our method could maintain around 90% SR of the full data setting. These strongly demonstrate the data efficiency of our method.

Few-shot Generalization Next, we test if our framework can generalize to novel compositional procedures with relatively supervised examples. We design the few-shot experiments where a subset of the executable procedural actions ($\boldsymbol{a}^e$) are held out, and we sample at most 20 samples of each

[4] Singh et al. (2020) predicts atomic navigation sequences (*e.g.*`MoveAhead`) instead of `Navigate`. The agent struggles to navigate to destination with only high-level goal. This shows the difficulty of navigation under our experiment setting.

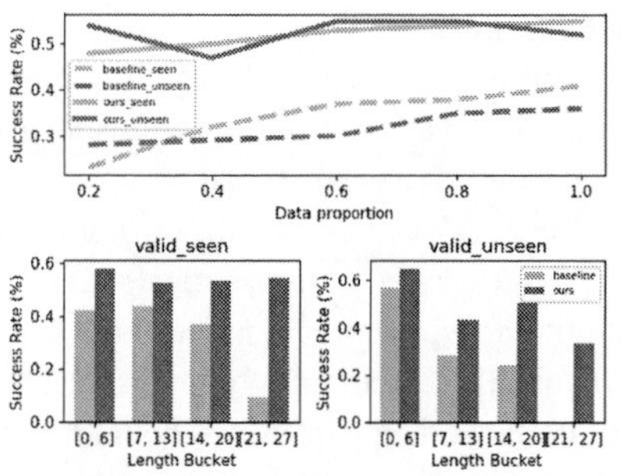

Figure 2: The SR (%) with proportions of the full training set (top) and on each length bucket of the *seen,unseen* (bottom).

$\boldsymbol{a}^e$ and add them to the training set. We evaluate the model on these held-out $\boldsymbol{a}^e$. We use two strategies to choose the held-out set; the first randomly selects n $\boldsymbol{a}^e$; the other selects the longest n $\boldsymbol{a}^e$ (n = 4/19). PaP-HMN achieves **33.1** and **44.9** SR with these two strategies while the reactive baseline only reaches 13.9 and 3.3 respectively[5]. Our method consistently outperforms the baseline by a large margin on both settings, which strongly demonstrates our method's generalization ability in the few-shot scenario. The significant gain under the short to long setting shows our method's strong capacities in completing long-horizon tasks in a data-efficient way compared to the baseline.

Analysis Our framework brings several advantages. First, compared to low-level actions, the high-level procedural functions are better aligned with abstract NL inputs. This thus benefits the learning and the prediction of PLANNER. Second, programs maintain the consistency of the actions, while a reactive agent might make inconsistent predictions, especially arguments, between actions. Finally, the modular design of PLANNER and the REACTORS improve the robust behavior of the agent. More discussion with examples is in §D.1.

Next, we investigate failure cases. First, our ablation study shows that PLANNER correctly predicts 80% of executable procedural actions $\boldsymbol{a}^e$, and the failures are mainly due to rare words (*e.g.* <u>*soak a plate*</u>). In addition, we manually annotated 50 failed examples whose $\boldsymbol{a}^e$ are correct. We found that 26 failures are due to the sub-optimal interaction positions of the receptacles that we compute during the pre-search phase (§C.1). This causes the interaction with a visible object or receptacle to fail. The pre-search map also missed some objects, and navigating to these objects always failed. Besides,

[5]For *random split*, we average over four different splits.

```
def udp_heat_object(obj):
    reactor = get_reactor("find_qualified_appliance")
    app = reactor(obj) # (e.g. microwave, oven)
    udp_navigation(app)
    atomic_reactor = get_reactor("predict_atomic_action")
    atomic_action = atomic_reactor(app)
    while atomic_action != STOP:
        env.call(atomic_action)
        atomic_action = atomic_reactor(app)
```

Table 7: A potential rewriting of **C1** of Tab. 3.

the REACTOR prediction errors fail on 18 examples; ambiguous annotations caused two errors, and the wrong argument prediction of the PLANNER caused four errors. §D.2 shows a comprehensive discussion with potential solutions.

8 Limitations and Future Work

Overall, our experiments demonstrate the benefit of our framework for encoding hierarchical procedural knowledge, especially under low-data or few-shot generalization regimes. One limitation of the experiments here is that they covered domains where it is relatively easy to enumerate the tasks that must be solved in the domain. One intuitive solution in situations where this is not possible is to manually create libraries that cover major procedures but fall back to atomic/reactive control when necessary. For example, as in Tab. 7, the program can call a reactor implemented as a the neural network (`atomic_reactor`) to predict atomic actions when using different appliance to heat an object, instead of enumerating different conditional branches. Another possibility is to automate procedure library creation through mining structured procedural knowledge from Web (Tenorth et al., 2010; Kunze et al., 2010), or through induction of high-level procedures from corpora of atomic action sequences (Ellis et al., 2020).

Another interesting note is that though hierarchical procedural knowledge is ubiquitous in human daily life, most existing NL instruction following benchmarks do not feature such complex, hierarchical procedures. Although there can be hierarchies embedded in vision-language navigation tasks (Anderson et al., 2018), game playing through reading documentation (Zhong et al., 2019) or through NL communication (Suhr et al., 2019; Jernite et al., 2019) and mobile phone navigation (Li et al., 2020), the hierarchies are shallow at best, or the occasional complex ones are limited in their breadth. Therefore, creating NL instruction following benchmarks that feature more realistic and diverse procedures is one final important direction for future work.

References

Peter Anderson, Qi Wu, Damien Teney, Jake Bruce, Mark Johnson, Niko Sünderhauf, Ian D. Reid, Stephen Gould, and Anton van den Hengel. 2018. Vision-and-language navigation: Interpreting visually-grounded navigation instructions in real environments. In *2018 IEEE Conference on Computer Vision and Pattern Recognition, CVPR 2018, Salt Lake City, UT, USA, June 18-22, 2018*, pages 3674–3683. IEEE Computer Society.

Jacob Andreas, Dan Klein, and Sergey Levine. 2017. Modular multitask reinforcement learning with policy sketches. In *Proceedings of the 34th International Conference on Machine Learning, ICML 2017, Sydney, NSW, Australia, 6-11 August 2017*, volume 70 of *Proceedings of Machine Learning Research*, pages 166–175. PMLR.

Jacob Andreas, Marcus Rohrbach, Trevor Darrell, and Dan Klein. 2016. Neural module networks. In *2016 IEEE Conference on Computer Vision and Pattern Recognition, CVPR 2016, Las Vegas, NV, USA, June 27-30, 2016*, pages 39–48. IEEE Computer Society.

Yoav Artzi, Dipanjan Das, and Slav Petrov. 2014. Learning compact lexicons for CCG semantic parsing. In *Proceedings of the 2014 Conference on Empirical Methods in Natural Language Processing (EMNLP)*, pages 1273–1283, Doha, Qatar. Association for Computational Linguistics.

Yoav Artzi and Luke Zettlemoyer. 2013. Weakly supervised learning of semantic parsers for mapping instructions to actions. *Transactions of the Association for Computational Linguistics*, 1:49–62.

Pierre-Luc Bacon, Jean Harb, and Doina Precup. 2017. The option-critic architecture. In *Proceedings of the Thirty-First AAAI Conference on Artificial Intelligence, February 4-9, 2017, San Francisco, California, USA*, pages 1726–1734. AAAI Press.

Dzmitry Bahdanau, Kyunghyun Cho, and Yoshua Bengio. 2015. Neural machine translation by jointly learning to align and translate. In *3rd International Conference on Learning Representations, ICLR 2015, San Diego, CA, USA, May 7-9, 2015, Conference Track Proceedings*.

David L. Chen and Raymond J. Mooney. 2011. Learning to interpret natural language navigation instructions from observations. In *Proceedings of the Twenty-Fifth AAAI Conference on Artificial Intelligence, AAAI 2011, San Francisco, California, USA, August 7-11, 2011*. AAAI Press.

Xinyun Chen, Chen Liang, Adams Wei Yu, Dawn Song, and Denny Zhou. 2020. Compositional generalization via neural-symbolic stack machines. In *Advances in Neural Information Processing Systems 33: Annual Conference on Neural Information Processing Systems 2020, NeurIPS 2020, December 6-12, 2020, virtual*.

Michele Colledanchise and Petter Ögren. 2018. *Behavior trees in robotics and AI: An introduction*. CRC Press.

Abhishek Das, Georgia Gkioxari, Stefan Lee, Devi Parikh, and Dhruv Batra. 2019. Neural Modular Control for Embodied Question Answering. *arXiv:1810.11181 [cs]*. ArXiv: 1810.11181.

Matt Deitke, Winson Han, Alvaro Herrasti, Aniruddha Kembhavi, Eric Kolve, Roozbeh Mottaghi, Jordi Salvador, Dustin Schwenk, Eli VanderBilt, Matthew Wallingford, Luca Weihs, Mark Yatskar, and Ali Farhadi. 2020. Robothor: An open simulation-to-real embodied AI platform. In *2020 IEEE/CVF Conference on Computer Vision and Pattern Recognition, CVPR 2020, Seattle, WA, USA, June 13-19, 2020*, pages 3161–3171. IEEE.

Kevin Ellis, Catherine Wong, Maxwell Nye, Mathias Sable-Meyer, Luc Cary, Lucas Morales, Luke Hewitt, Armando Solar-Lezama, and Joshua B Tenenbaum. 2020. Dreamcoder: Growing generalizable, interpretable knowledge with wake-sleep bayesian program learning. *arXiv preprint arXiv:2006.08381*.

Richard E Fikes and Nils J Nilsson. 1971. Strips: A new approach to the application of theorem proving to problem solving. *Artificial intelligence*, 2(3-4):189–208.

Alexander L. Gaunt, Marc Brockschmidt, Nate Kushman, and Daniel Tarlow. 2017. Differentiable programs with neural libraries. In *Proceedings of the 34th International Conference on Machine Learning, ICML 2017, Sydney, NSW, Australia, 6-11 August 2017*, volume 70 of *Proceedings of Machine Learning Research*, pages 1213–1222. PMLR.

Daniel Gordon, Aniruddha Kembhavi, Mohammad Rastegari, Joseph Redmon, Dieter Fox, and Ali Farhadi. 2018. IQA: visual question answering in interactive environments. In *2018 IEEE Conference on Computer Vision and Pattern Recognition, CVPR 2018, Salt Lake City, UT, USA, June 18-22, 2018*, pages 4089–4098. IEEE Computer Society.

Saurabh Gupta, James Davidson, Sergey Levine, Rahul Sukthankar, and Jitendra Malik. 2017. Cognitive mapping and planning for visual navigation. In *2017 IEEE Conference on Computer Vision and Pattern Recognition, CVPR 2017, Honolulu, HI, USA, July 21-26, 2017*, pages 7272–7281. IEEE Computer Society.

Kaiming He, Georgia Gkioxari, Piotr Dollár, and Ross B. Girshick. 2017. Mask R-CNN. In *IEEE International Conference on Computer Vision, ICCV 2017, Venice, Italy, October 22-29, 2017*, pages 2980–2988. IEEE Computer Society.

Kaiming He, Xiangyu Zhang, Shaoqing Ren, and Jian Sun. 2016. Deep residual learning for image recognition. In *2016 IEEE Conference on Computer Vi-*

sion and Pattern Recognition, CVPR 2016, Las Vegas, NV, USA, June 27-30, 2016, pages 770–778. IEEE Computer Society.

Hengyuan Hu, Denis Yarats, Qucheng Gong, Yuandong Tian, and Mike Lewis. 2019. Hierarchical decision making by generating and following natural language instructions. In *Advances in Neural Information Processing Systems 32: Annual Conference on Neural Information Processing Systems 2019, NeurIPS 2019, December 8-14, 2019, Vancouver, BC, Canada*, pages 10025–10034.

Srinivasan Iyer, Alvin Cheung, and Luke Zettlemoyer. 2019. Learning programmatic idioms for scalable semantic parsing. In *Proceedings of the 2019 Conference on Empirical Methods in Natural Language Processing and the 9th International Joint Conference on Natural Language Processing (EMNLP-IJCNLP)*, pages 5426–5435, Hong Kong, China. Association for Computational Linguistics.

Srinivasan Iyer, Ioannis Konstas, Alvin Cheung, Jayant Krishnamurthy, and Luke Zettlemoyer. 2017. Learning a neural semantic parser from user feedback. In *Proceedings of the 55th Annual Meeting of the Association for Computational Linguistics (Volume 1: Long Papers)*, pages 963–973, Vancouver, Canada. Association for Computational Linguistics.

Yacine Jernite, Kavya Srinet, Jonathan Gray, and Arthur Szlam. 2019. CraftAssist Instruction Parsing: Semantic Parsing for a Minecraft Assistant. *arXiv:1905.01978 [cs]*. ArXiv: 1905.01978.

Yiding Jiang, Shixiang Gu, Kevin Murphy, and Chelsea Finn. 2019a. Language as an abstraction for hierarchical deep reinforcement learning. In *Advances in Neural Information Processing Systems 32: Annual Conference on Neural Information Processing Systems 2019, NeurIPS 2019, December 8-14, 2019, Vancouver, BC, Canada*, pages 9414–9426.

Yu-qian Jiang, Shi-qi Zhang, Piyush Khandelwal, and Peter Stone. 2019b. Task planning in robotics: an empirical comparison of pddl-and asp-based systems. *Frontiers of Information Technology & Electronic Engineering*, 20(3):363–373.

Leslie Pack Kaelbling and Tomás Lozano-Pérez. 2011. Hierarchical task and motion planning in the now. In *2011 IEEE International Conference on Robotics and Automation*, pages 1470–1477. IEEE.

Siddharth Karamcheti, Dorsa Sadigh, and Percy Liang. 2020. Learning adaptive language interfaces through decomposition. In *Proceedings of the First Workshop on Interactive and Executable Semantic Parsing*, pages 23–33, Online. Association for Computational Linguistics.

Diederik P. Kingma and Jimmy Ba. 2015. Adam: A method for stochastic optimization. In *3rd International Conference on Learning Representations, ICLR 2015, San Diego, CA, USA, May 7-9, 2015, Conference Track Proceedings*.

Lars Kunze, Moritz Tenorth, and Michael Beetz. 2010. Putting people's common sense into knowledge bases of household robots. In *Annual Conference on Artificial Intelligence*, pages 151–159. Springer.

Yang Li, Jiacong He, Xin Zhou, Yuan Zhang, and Jason Baldridge. 2020. Mapping natural language instructions to mobile UI action sequences. In *Proceedings of the 58th Annual Meeting of the Association for Computational Linguistics*, pages 8198–8210, Online. Association for Computational Linguistics.

Yuan-Hong Liao, Xavier Puig, Marko Boben, Antonio Torralba, and Sanja Fidler. 2019. Synthesizing environment-aware activities via activity sketches. In *IEEE Conference on Computer Vision and Pattern Recognition, CVPR 2019, Long Beach, CA, USA, June 16-20, 2019*, pages 6291–6299. Computer Vision Foundation / IEEE.

Tsung-Yi Lin, Michael Maire, Serge Belongie, James Hays, Pietro Perona, Deva Ramanan, Piotr Dollár, and C Lawrence Zitnick. 2014. Microsoft coco: Common objects in context. In *European conference on computer vision*, pages 740–755. Springer.

Chih-Yao Ma, Jiasen Lu, Zuxuan Wu, Ghassan AlRegib, Zsolt Kira, Richard Socher, and Caiming Xiong. 2019. Self-monitoring navigation agent via auxiliary progress estimation. In *7th International Conference on Learning Representations, ICLR 2019, New Orleans, LA, USA, May 6-9, 2019*. OpenReview.net.

Dipendra Misra, Andrew Bennett, Valts Blukis, Eyvind Niklasson, Max Shatkhin, and Yoav Artzi. 2018. Mapping instructions to actions in 3D environments with visual goal prediction. In *Proceedings of the 2018 Conference on Empirical Methods in Natural Language Processing*, pages 2667–2678, Brussels, Belgium. Association for Computational Linguistics.

Dipendra K Misra, Jaeyong Sung, Kevin Lee, and Ashutosh Saxena. 2016. Tell me dave: Context-sensitive grounding of natural language to manipulation instructions. *The International Journal of Robotics Research*, 35(1-3):281–300.

Xavier Puig, Kevin Ra, Marko Boben, Jiaman Li, Tingwu Wang, Sanja Fidler, and Antonio Torralba. 2018. Virtualhome: Simulating household activities via programs. In *2018 IEEE Conference on Computer Vision and Pattern Recognition, CVPR 2018, Salt Lake City, UT, USA, June 18-22, 2018*, pages 8494–8502. IEEE Computer Society.

Maxim Rabinovich, Mitchell Stern, and Dan Klein. 2017. Abstract syntax networks for code generation and semantic parsing. In *Proceedings of the 55th Annual Meeting of the Association for Computational Linguistics (Volume 1: Long Papers)*, pages 1139–1149, Vancouver, Canada. Association for Computational Linguistics.

Mukund Raghothaman, Y. Wei, and Y. Hamadi. 2016. Swim: Synthesizing what i mean - code search and idiomatic snippet synthesis. *2016 IEEE/ACM 38th International Conference on Software Engineering (ICSE)*, pages 357–367.

Joseph Redmon and Ali Farhadi. 2018. Yolov3: An incremental improvement. *arXiv preprint arXiv:1804.02767*.

Eui Chul Richard Shin, Miltiadis Allamanis, Marc Brockschmidt, and Alex Polozov. 2019. Program synthesis and semantic parsing with learned code idioms. In *Advances in Neural Information Processing Systems 32: Annual Conference on Neural Information Processing Systems 2019, NeurIPS 2019, December 8-14, 2019, Vancouver, BC, Canada*, pages 10824–10834.

Mohit Shridhar, Jesse Thomason, Daniel Gordon, Yonatan Bisk, Winson Han, Roozbeh Mottaghi, Luke Zettlemoyer, and Dieter Fox. 2020a. ALFRED: A benchmark for interpreting grounded instructions for everyday tasks. In *2020 IEEE/CVF Conference on Computer Vision and Pattern Recognition, CVPR 2020, Seattle, WA, USA, June 13-19, 2020*, pages 10737–10746. IEEE.

Mohit Shridhar, Xingdi Yuan, Marc-Alexandre Côté, Yonatan Bisk, Adam Trischler, and Matthew Hausknecht. 2020b. ALFWorld: Aligning Text and Embodied Environments for Interactive Learning. *arXiv:2010.03768 [cs]*. ArXiv: 2010.03768.

Kunal Pratap Singh, Suvaansh Bhambri, Byeonghwi Kim, Roozbeh Mottaghi, and Jonghyun Choi. 2020. Moca: A modular object-centric approach for interactive instruction following. *arXiv preprint arXiv:2012.03208*.

Siddharth Srivastava, Eugene Fang, Lorenzo Riano, Rohan Chitnis, Stuart Russell, and Pieter Abbeel. 2014. Combined task and motion planning through an extensible planner-independent interface layer. In *2014 IEEE international conference on robotics and automation (ICRA)*, pages 639–646. IEEE.

Siddharth Srivastava, Lorenzo Riano, Stuart Russell, and Pieter Abbeel. 2013. Using classical planners for tasks with continuous operators in robotics. In *Intl. Conf. on Automated Planning and Scheduling*, volume 3. Citeseer.

Alane Suhr, Claudia Yan, Jack Schluger, Stanley Yu, Hadi Khader, Marwa Mouallem, Iris Zhang, and Yoav Artzi. 2019. Executing instructions in situated collaborative interactions. In *Proceedings of the 2019 Conference on Empirical Methods in Natural Language Processing and the 9th International Joint Conference on Natural Language Processing (EMNLP-IJCNLP)*, pages 2119–2130, Hong Kong, China. Association for Computational Linguistics.

Shao-Hua Sun, Te-Lin Wu, and Joseph J. Lim. 2020. Program guided agent. In *8th International Conference on Learning Representations, ICLR 2020, Addis Ababa, Ethiopia, April 26-30, 2020*. OpenReview.net.

Richard S Sutton, Doina Precup, and Satinder Singh. 1999. Between mdps and semi-mdps: A framework for temporal abstraction in reinforcement learning. *Artificial intelligence*, 112(1-2):181–211.

Moritz Tenorth, Daniel Nyga, and Michael Beetz. 2010. Understanding and executing instructions for everyday manipulation tasks from the World Wide Web. In *2010 IEEE International Conference on Robotics and Automation*, pages 1486–1491, Anchorage, AK. IEEE.

Oriol Vinyals, Meire Fortunato, and Navdeep Jaitly. 2015. Pointer networks. In *Advances in Neural Information Processing Systems 28: Annual Conference on Neural Information Processing Systems 2015, December 7-12, 2015, Montreal, Quebec, Canada*, pages 2692–2700.

Jiajun Wu, Erika Lu, Pushmeet Kohli, Bill Freeman, and Josh Tenenbaum. 2017. Learning to see physics via visual de-animation. In *Advances in Neural Information Processing Systems 30: Annual Conference on Neural Information Processing Systems 2017, December 4-9, 2017, Long Beach, CA, USA*, pages 153–164.

Nancy Xu, Sam Masling, Michael Du, Giovanni Campagna, Larry Heck, James Landay, and Monica Lam. 2021. Grounding open-domain instructions to automate web support tasks. In *Proceedings of the 2021 Conference of the North American Chapter of the Association for Computational Linguistics: Human Language Technologies*, pages 1022–1032, Online. Association for Computational Linguistics.

Pengcheng Yin and Graham Neubig. 2017. A syntactic neural model for general-purpose code generation. In *Proceedings of the 55th Annual Meeting of the Association for Computational Linguistics (Volume 1: Long Papers)*, pages 440–450, Vancouver, Canada. Association for Computational Linguistics.

Licheng Yu, Xinlei Chen, Georgia Gkioxari, Mohit Bansal, Tamara L. Berg, and Dhruv Batra. 2019. Multi-target embodied question answering. In *IEEE Conference on Computer Vision and Pattern Recognition, CVPR 2019, Long Beach, CA, USA, June 16-20, 2019*, pages 6309–6318. Computer Vision Foundation / IEEE.

Tao Yu, Rui Zhang, Kai Yang, Michihiro Yasunaga, Dongxu Wang, Zifan Li, James Ma, Irene Li, Qingning Yao, Shanelle Roman, Zilin Zhang, and Dragomir Radev. 2018. Spider: A large-scale human-labeled dataset for complex and cross-domain semantic parsing and text-to-SQL task. In *Proceedings of the 2018 Conference on Empirical Methods in Natural Language Processing*, pages 3911–3921, Brussels, Belgium. Association for Computational Linguistics.

Luke Zettlemoyer and M. Collins. 2005. Learning to map sentences to logical form: Structured classification with probabilistic categorial grammars. In *UAI*.

Victor Zhong, Tim Rocktäschel, and Edward Grefenstette. 2019. Rtfm: Generalising to novel environment dynamics via reading. *arXiv preprint arXiv:1910.08210*.

Victor Zhong, Caiming Xiong, and R. Socher. 2017. Seq2sql: Generating structured queries from natural language using reinforcement learning. *ArXiv*, abs/1709.00103.

Fengda Zhu, Yi Zhu, Xiaojun Chang, and Xiaodan Liang. 2020. Vision-language navigation with self-supervised auxiliary reasoning tasks. In *2020 IEEE/CVF Conference on Computer Vision and Pattern Recognition, CVPR 2020, Seattle, WA, USA, June 13-19, 2020*, pages 10009–10019. IEEE.

A Full Procedural Library

The full procedural library for IQA is listed in Tab. 9 and that for ALFRED is listed in Tab. 10.

B User-issued Procedural Library

Fig. 3 shows the screenshot of the annotation guideline. We purposefully avoid any dataset-related examples. The programmer takes around 90 minutes to complete the annotation. The procedural library created by a programmer without prior knowledge to the ALFRED dataset is in Tab. 11. The programmer could issue reasonable procedural functions that highly resemble our own creations. The reactors can be added to detect the properties of the objects before the condition clauses.

C Experiment Settings

In this section of the appendix, we describe the detailed implementation of the pre-search map, the heuristic induction of supervisions from existing annotation of the AFLFRED dataset and the implementation of the baseline and our HMN for reproduce purpose.

C.1 Pre-search Map Procedure

We treat each scene as a grid map with grid size 0.25. The agent stands on each point, turn around 90 degrees a time and move its camera with degree [-30, 0, 30] and scan. The best position for a receptacle satisfy (1) the agent can open/close the receptacle, can pick up/put an object from/to it. (2) the visual area of the receptacle is the largest compared to other positions. A threshold is used to avoid standing too closed. For ALFRED only, we record the positions of movable objects (*e.g.* apple). This is done by enumerating all the receptacle positions, open them if needed and select the receptacle position that makes the object most visible.

The map creation also requires an object detection model to detect objects for each scan. For IQA, we use the fine-tuned YOLO-v3 detector as describe in §6.1 and the area of an object is calculated by its bounding box. For ALFRED, we instead use an oracle object detector to minimize the pre-search performance loss.

Notably, there are many existing works that apply the similar replacement (Shridhar et al., 2020b; Karamcheti et al., 2020). For example, Shridhar et al. (2020b) pre-search the map, records the coordinates of each object and uses an A* planner to navigate between two positions. This replacement that allows the agent to proceed to a location without fail.

C.2 Reactive Baseline

IQA The reactive baseline is implemented as a pointer network (Vinyals et al., 2015) whose output sequence corresponds to the positions in an input sequence. To make a fair comparison with our method, we provide this baseline with the available receptacle IDs of each scene, the question type, and the targeted objects. For instance, given the question *how many mugs in the fridge* for scene i, we list all the receptacles (*e.g.* fridge_1, cabinet_2) in the order of distance to the agent's initial position as well as the question type "contains" and the two working objects "mug" and "fridge". The fixed set of actions and the answers are added at the beginning of the input so that the model does not need an extra generation component. The reactive agent needs to navigate to each receptacle, operate them properly and generate an answer at the end. The images are encoded and the objects are detected with the same YOLO-v3 detector as in HMN.

While an action sequence is not provided in the release of the dataset, we heuristically create such action sequences by enumerating the input receptacle list of each sample. The size for each question type is 7000 and a total of 21000 samples are used in the training. We additionally compare with the HIMN proposed in Gordon et al. (2018) that designs a meta-controller that calls different controllers to accomplish different tasks (*e.g.* navigation, manipulation), and an A3C agent implemented in the same work.

ALFRED We follow Shridhar et al. (2020a) to setup our reactive baseline. This baseline takes the natural language instruction x as input, then it predicts an atomic action at each time step, conditioned on the vision, the previous generated atomic action, and the attended language. The baseline also has a progress monitor component to track the task completion progress (Ma et al., 2019). We make the same replacement of the atomic navigation actions with `Navigate destination`. The original mask generator is replaced by the same Mask R-CNN used in our HMN.

For both datasets, we use `seen` and `unseen` validation set for the evaluation. The floorplans of the `unseen` split are held-out in the training data. Each floorplan defines the appearance of the environment as well as the arrangement of the objects.

Annotation Guideline

Assuming you are creating a library written in Python that could be used to *describe how to accomplish a set of tasks.*

To understand the tasks, you are given 7 task categories and in each category, you are given 3 trajectories to achieve a specific goal stated as natural language. Each trajectory consists of a sequence of *atomic actions(e.g. GotoLocation)* and their *arguments(e.g. Desktop)*.

One key feature of the function you create is **reusable**. For example, if an action sequence (e.g. atomic_action_1, atomic_action_2 and atomic_action_3) is frequently observed, you can compose super_action_1 that consists of these three actions. In addition, you can use any composed super_action to compose other super_actions. For example, if there is a super_action_2 that consists of atomic_action_1, atomic_action_2 and atomic_action_3 and atomic_action_4, you can define this super_action_2 as super_action_1, atomic_action_4. Their corresponding Python functions are listed below. You can freely name the arguments, which can be as simple as 'object_1', 'object_2'

```
def super_action_1(arg1, arg2):
        atomic_action_1(arg1)
        atomic_action_2(arg2)
        atomic_action_3(arg2)

def super_action_2(arg1, arg2):
        super_action_1(args1, args2)
        atomic_action_4(arg2)
```

Another key feature of the function you create is **good coverage/generalizable**. As in your daily life, you can take different actions to accomplish the same goal. The different action might be due to the diverse nature of accomplishing the task (e.g. you can either order online or go to a local supermarket to buy some food). Or it is due to the dynamic environment (e.g. when you buy the food in the supermarket that only accepts cash, you have to withdraw money if you don't have any, but you can skip this withdrawal process if you have cash with you). This is defined through conditions

```
def shop_in_super_market:
        if not_have_cash:
                withdraw_cash()
        # shopping, a super_action
        super_action_i()
```

The reason why we treat this function as a more generalizable function is that, if you do not write in this way, you will have to compose two distinct functions even though they achieve the same goal in the end:

```
def shop_in_super_market_with_cash:
        # shopping

def shop_in_super_market_without_cash:
        withdraw_cash()
        # shopping
```

Figure 3: The annotation guideline for a programmer to create procedural functions with 21 examples from the ALFRED dataset.

For IQA, we measure the answer accuracy, and we follow Shridhar et al. (2020a) to measure the task success rate (SR), which defines the percentage of whole task completion; and sub-task success rate (SSR), which measures the ratio of individual sub-task completion for ALFRED.

C.3 HMN Implementation

IQA Since the natural language questions x are generated with a limited number of templates, we use a rule-based HMN-PLANNER that recognizes each template and classifies a template to one of the three question types whose corresponding procedural actions are listed as the top three functions in Tab. 9.

We model the two reactors ATTRCHECKER and RELCHECKER as two multi-classes classifiers. We first follow Gordon et al. (2018) to use a YOLO-v3 (Redmon and Farhadi, 2018) that is fine-tuned on the images sampled from THOR for object detection. This object detector scan each visual input and generate a bounding box and a class name for each detected object. Since there are only seven receptacles, the ATTRCHECKER uses the predicted class name of a receptacle to decide whether the receptacle is openable or not. It then marks the receptacle as is_open=True after the atomic open action is launched for the receptacle. The RELCHECKER use bounding box to heuristically decide the spatial relation between an object and a receptacle. The RELCHECKER considers that an object is inside a receptacle if its bounding box has over 70% overlap with the receptacle's bounding box.

ALFRED We use a sequence-to-sequence model with attention (Bahdanau et al., 2015) as our PLANNER. The input to the encoder is the natural language x. The decoder generates one function a_i at a time from a constrained vocabulary

$\mathcal{A}^p \bigcup \mathcal{A}^a$, conditioned on x and the action history $\{a_1, ..., a_{i-1}\}$.

We adopt the pre-trained Mask R-CNN (He et al., 2017) that is fine-tuned on the ALFRED dataset from Shridhar et al. (2020b) as our MGENERATOR. It returns the name and the bounding box for all detected objects in the visual input. Its parameters are frozen. We design ATTRCHECKER and REFINDER as two multi-classes classifiers. The inputs to these two reactors are the object name $\boldsymbol{h}^o$ encoded by a BI-LSTM, the immediate vision $\boldsymbol{h}^i$ encoded by a frozen RESNET-18 CNN (He et al., 2016) following Shridhar et al. (2020a), the called action sequence $\boldsymbol{h}^a$ encoded with a LSTM and the attended input $\boldsymbol{h}^l$ with $\boldsymbol{h}^a$. These four vectors are concatenated together as $\boldsymbol{h}^f$. A fully connected layer and a non-linear activation function are added to predict class probabilities.

C.4 AFLRED Supervision Induction

We induced the ground truth labels for each component of the HMN from ALFRED with the help of atomic action sequences and the subgoal sequences provided by the dataset so that the HMN can be trained in a supervised fashion to maximize the log-likelihood of the label. First, we used the subgoal sequences to annotate the executable procedural actions for the planner. For example, a subgoal sequence `Goto`, `Pick`, `Clean`, `Goto`, `Put` was annotated with `udp_clean_object`, `udp_put_object`. A different subgoal sequence `Goto`, `Pickup`, `Goto Clean`, `Put` was annotated with the same procedural action sequence. The first author annotated 30 most frequent subgoal sequences of the training set of ALFRED and resulted in 19 different executable procedural actions[6]. Next, we used the atomic action sequences of the dataset to generate the labels for the reactors. For example, if there is an `Open` before a `Pickup` in the atomic action sequence, the attribute of the corresponding object is labeled as openable=True and is_open=False.

When doing the sanity check to verify the coverage of our created procedural library, we assign an executable procedural action $\boldsymbol{a}^e$ to each sample, we then check whether the atomic action sequence of $\boldsymbol{a}^e$ match the annotated atomic action sequence provided by the dataset. Unmatched examples are reviewed and the procedural library is updated as in §6.2.

[6]We discarded a training example if its subgoal sequence is not annotated with the procedure library. About 500 samples among 21k training data are discarded.

C.5 Hyperparameters

IQA Baseline The embedding size is 100, the hidden size of the BI-LSTM and LSTM are 256 and 512. We take the same three feature vectors before the YOLO detection layer and convert the channel size to 32 with convolution layers to encode an image. The flatted features are concatenated with dropout rate of 0.5. We use Adam (Kingma and Ba, 2015) with learning rate 1e-4.

ALFRED We follow Shridhar et al. (2020a) for the hyperparameter selection of the baseline and our model if they are applicable (*e.g.* embedding size, optimizer). We observe that training longer yields better task completion, and thus we train the baseline for 15 epochs and ours for 10 epochs. For our method only, the size of $\boldsymbol{h}^o$, $\boldsymbol{h}^a$ and $\boldsymbol{h}^l$ is 512. The activation function of ATTRCHECKER is Sigmoid and the output size is 3 (*i.e.* is_openable, is_open, is_close). The activation function of REFINDER is Softmax and the output size equals the object vocabulary size.

D Analysis

In this section, we present concrete examples to demonstrate the benefit of our proposed pipeline. We also show a few failures of our pipeline to encourage future developments.

D.1 Advantage of HMN

The above results suggest that our proposed framework with modularized task-specific components and predefined procedure knowledge is effective in controlling situated agents via complex natural language commands. Compared with the reactive agent, this framework brings several benefits. First, instead of directly controlling an agent using low-level atomic actions, it predicts holistic procedural programs, which are better aligned with high-level input NL descriptions. For instance, in Examples 1 and 2 in Tab. 8, common NL phrases like *put · in ·* naturally map to the procedure `udp_pick_put_object`, while the reactive baseline could struggle at interpreting the correspondence between the NL intents and the verbose low-level atomic actions, resulting in incomplete predictions. Second, using procedures could help maintain *consistency* of actions. Specifically, given a procedure (*e.g.*`udp_pick_put_object`), and its

Task: Put a chilled egg in the sink **Reactive:** Navigate **egg** Pickup **egg** Navigate **fridge** Open **fridge** STOP **HMN-PLANNER:** udp_cool_object(egg), udp_pick_put_object(egg, sink)
Task: Put CDs in a safe. (*requires to put *two* CDs) **Reactive:** Navigate **cd** Pickup **cd** Navigate **safe** Open **safe** Put **cd safe** Close **safe** STOP **HMN-PLANNER:** udp_pick_put_object(cd, safe), udp_pick_put_object(cd, safe)
Task: Place a cooked potato slice in the fridge **Reactive:** Navigate **knife** Pickup **knife** Navigate **potato** Slice **potato** Navigate **fridge** Put **knife countertop** Navigate **potato** Close **potato** ... **HMN-PLANNER:** udp_slice_object(potato), udp_heat_object(potato), udp_pick_and_put(potato, fridge)

Table 8: Common failures of the reactive baseline. All actions of the reactive baseline are atomic actions.

arguments (*e.g.*knife, fridge), the HMN agent is guaranteed to coherently carry out the specified action without being interfered, while the reactive baseline could predict inconsistent atomic actions in-between (*e.g.* the underscored arguments of Navigate and Put should be the same in Example 3). Finally, we remark that procedures also improve the robust behavior of the agent. For instance, when interacting with container objects (*e.g.* fridge), HMN would call the dedicated ATTRCHECKER to decide whether to open the object first (*e.g.* C4,Fig. 1), and it mis-predicts once, while the reactive baseline fails to perform the Open action 33 times on the *unseen* split.

D.2 Error Analysis

We first did an ablation study on the PLANNER on the *unseen* split. PLANNER correctly predicts 80% executable procedural actions $\boldsymbol{a}^e$, and the failures are mainly due to rare words in utterances (*e.g.* <u>soak</u> *a plate*. Next, we manually annotated 50 failed examples among samples whose $\boldsymbol{a}^e$ are correctly predicted by the PLANNER. We found that 26 failures are due to the sub-optimal interaction positions of the receptacles that we compute during the pre-search phase (§C.1). This results in the failures of putting an object in-hand to a visible receptacle or picking up a visible object. The pre-search map also missed some objects and navigating to these objects always failed. This problem can be alleviated either by adding additional procedural actions to move around and attempt to pick up or put an object until success, or by doing more careful engineering to create the map. Additionally, 18 examples are caused by prediction errors of reactors. For instance, REFINDER could given incorrect predictions of the containing receptacle of an object. The receptacle is not correctly operated before the targeted object is visible. While such errors are inevitable due to imperfect reactors, it could be potentially mitigated by designing more robust procedures, *e.g.*, enumerating over the top-n most likely receptacles for a target object instead of the best scored one by the reactor. Other approaches, like introducing object-centric representations to the reactors (Wu et al., 2017; Singh et al., 2020), could also be helpful. The remainder of the errors are caused by ambiguous annotation (2 examples), and wrong argument predictions of the planner (4 examples).

E Related Work

Procedure-guided Learning The idea of using predefined procedures for agent control has been explored in the literature. For example, Andreas et al. (2017); Das et al. (2019) use high-level symbolic program sketches to guide an agent's exploration; Gordon et al. (2018); Yu et al. (2019) design meta-controller to call different low-level controllers. There only exists one explicit level of the hierarchy. Sun et al. (2020) show that programs can assist agent's task completions. They require the presence of the program for each task, while our programs are generated by the planner. There is no nested function in their provided programs too. Programs are used to represent procedures in Puig et al. (2018), but no hierarchy is considered. Later Liao et al. (2019) annotate the dataset with program sketches and propose a graph-based method to generate executable programs. Their work requires a fully observed environment while we only consider egocentric visions. Recent works also explore representing hierarchies with natural language (Hu et al., 2019; Jiang et al., 2019a) and visual goal representation (Misra et al., 2018) instead of symbols. Another related area is probabilistic programming, where procedures serve as symbolic scaffolds to define the control flow of learnable programs (Gaunt et al., 2017). Our work is related to these research in using predefined procedural knowledge to assist learning, while we focus on leveraging such procedures to synthesize executable programs from natural language commands.

Semantic Parsing Our work is also related to semantic parsing, where executable programs are generated from natural language inputs. This includes mapping NL to domain-specific logical forms (*e.g.* lambda calculus, (Zettlemoyer and Collins, 2005)) or programs (*e.g.* SQL, (Zhong et al., 2017; Yu et al., 2018)). Recently there has also been a burgeoning of developing models that could transduce natural language intents into general-purpose programs (*e.g.* Python, (Yin and Neubig, 2017; Rabinovich et al., 2017)). Our work also considers program generation from NL, with a focus on the command and control of situated agents.

Research in semantic parsing has also explored leveraging idiomatic program structures, which are fragments of programs that frequently appear in training data, to aid generation (Raghothaman et al., 2016). Such idiomatic programs are mined from corpora (Iyer et al., 2019; Shin et al., 2019). Our work focuses on designing flexible and idiomatic procedures which interact with situated components (*e.g.* reactors) to adapt to environment-specific situations. This work also uses manually-curated procedures, because in our problem setting we do not have a readily available corpus of high-level procedural programs to automatically collect such idioms. We leave extracting procedures from low-level atomic actions as interesting future work.

Robotics Planning and Hierarchical Control Our procedure library shares the design philosophy with the macro-actions in the STRIPS representation in the robotics planning (Fikes and Nilsson, 1971). However, we do not define the pre-condition and the post-effect of the actions, and instead leave the models to learn the consequences. The task-level planning has been studied extensively (Kaelbling and Lozano-Pérez, 2011; Srivastava et al., 2013, 2014). These methods often work with high-level formal languages in low-dimensional state space, and they are typically designed for a specific environment and task. Our framework can be applied to various tasks and only partial observations are required. Previous works also leverage PDDL and the answer set planner (ASP) for task planning. PDDL+ASP is conceptually different from our formalism. PDDL+ASP aims at planning the actual execution sequences. The PDDL planner searches the action sequences based on the initial and the final state. Meanwhile, our formalism focuses on describing the procedure to accomplish a task. We use the HMN-Planner to predict the executable procedure sequence given the NL. It is possible to integrate them into one system. E.g.,a procedure function can call a PDDL planner if the pre/post conditions are clearer given NL. Finally, many works design mechanism to learn hierarchies automatically from supervisions of only the end-task (Sutton et al., 1999; Bacon et al., 2017), which might suffer from collapsing to trivial atomic actions.

```
# check the existence of an object in the scene
def udp_check_obj_exist(obj):
    all_recep = udp_grid_search_recep()
    for recep in all_recep:
        rel = udp_check_relation(obj, recep)
        if rel == OBJ_IN_RECEP:
            return True
    return False

# check whether a receptacle contains an object
def udp_check_contain(obj, recep):
    all_recep = \
    udp_grid_search_tar_recep(recep.desc)
    for recep in all_recep:
        rel = udp_check_relation(obj, recep)
        if rel == OBJ_IN_RECEP:
            return True
    return False

# count how many objects in the scene
def udp_count_obj(obj):
    tot = 0
    all_recep = udp_grid_search_recep()
    for recep in all_recep:
        rel = udp_check_relation(obj, recep)
        tot += int(rel == OBJ_IN_RECEP)
    return tot

# check object inside receptacle
def udp_check_relation(obj, recep):
    atomic_navigate(recep)
    r1 = get_reactor("check_obj_attr")
    r2 = get_reactor("check_obj_recep_rel")
    attr = r1(recep)
    if attr.is_openable and attr.is_closed:
        atomic_open_object(recep)
        rel = r2(obj, recep)
        atomic_close_object(recep)
    else:
        rel = r2(obj, recep)
    return rel

# get a list of target receptacles
def udp_grid_search_tar_recep(desc):
    recep_list = udp_grid_search_recep()
    tar_recep_list = [x for x in recep_list \\
    if x.desc == desc]
    return tar_recep_list
# navigate and search at every reachable points
def udp_grid_search_recep():
    if not done_search:
        all_receps = [] # global var
        for pos in reachable_pos:
            atomic_navigate_pos(pos)
            all_receps += udp_search_recep()
    return all_receps
```

Table 9: Procedural functions defined for IQA

```
# close an object if it is open
def udp_close_if_needed(obj):
    reactor = get_reactor("check_obj_attr")
    attr = reactor(obj)
    if attr.is_openable and attr.is_open:
        atomic_close_object(obj)
# "postpare" the receptacle
def udp_postpare_recep(obj):
    reactor = get_reactor("check_obj_attr")
    attr = reactor(obj)
    if attr.is_openable and attr.is_open:
        atomic_close_object(obj)
# pickup an object
def udp_pick_object(obj):
    reactor = get_reactor("find_obj_recep")
    udp_navigation(obj)
    recep = reactor(obj)
    udp_prepare_recep(recep)
    # this is for pickup laptop only
    udp_close_if_needed(obj)
    atomic_pick_object(obj)
    udp_postpare_recep(recep
# put an object to a receptacle
def udp_put_object(obj, dst):
    udp_navigation(dst)
    udp_prepare_recep(dst)
    atomic_put_object(obj, dst)
    udp_postpare_recep(dst)
# clean an object in the fauucet
def udp_clean_object(obj):
    # sink and faucet are global variables
    udp_pick_object(obj)
    udp_put_object(obj, sink)
    atomic_toggleon_object(faucet)
    atomic_toggleoff_object(faucet)
    udp_pick_object(obj)
# slice an object with a knife
def udp_slice_object(obj, tool_dst):
    # knife is a global variable
    udp_pick_object(knife)
    udp_navigation(obj)
    reactor = get_reactor("find_obj_recep")
    recep = reactor(obj)
    udp_prepare_recep(recep)
    atomic_slice_object(obj)
    udp_postpare_recep(recep)
    udp_put_object(tool, tool_dst)
# pick an object and then put it to a receptacle
def udp_pick_and_put_object(obj, dst):
    udp_pick_object(obj)
    udp_put_object(obj, dst)
# cool an object with fridge
def udp_cool_object(obj):
    # fridge is a global variable
    udp_pick_and_put_object(obj, fridge)
# heat an object with microwave
def udp_heat_object(obj):
    udp_pick_and_put_object(obj, microwave)
    atomic_toggleon_object(microwave)
# prepare a receptacle for interaction
def udp_prepare_recep(obj):
    reactor = get_reactor("check_obj_attr")
    attr = reactor(obj)
    if attr.is_openable and attr.is_closed:
        atomic_open_object(obj)
```

Table 10: Procedural functions defined for ALFRED

```
# udp_pick_object(obj):
def udp_pick_up(object, loc):
    udp_navigation(loc)
    if loc.is_open:
        atomic_pickup_object(object)
    else:
        atomic_open_object(loc)
        atomic_pickup_object(object)
        atomic_close_object(loc)

def udp_pick_up_to(object, loc, loc_to):
    udp_pick_up(object, loc)
    udp_navigation(loc_to)

# udp_put_object(obj, dst):
def udp_put_to(object, loc_to):
    udp_navigation(loc_to)
    if loc.is_open:
        PutObject(object)
    else:
        atomic_open_object(loc_to)
        atomic_put_object(loc_to)
        atomic_close_object(loc_to)

# udp_pick_and_put_object(obj, dst):
def udp_pick_put_to(object, loc, storage):
    udp_pick_up(object, loc)
    udp_put_to(object, storage)

def udp_look_under_light(object, loc, light_source):
    udp_pick_up_to(object, loc, light_source)
    atomic_toggleon_object(light_source)

# udp_slice_object(obj, tool_dst):
def udp_slice(object, loc, slicer):
    udp_pick_up_to(slicer, loc, object)
    atomic_slice_object(object)

def udp_toggle(object):
    atomic_toggleon_object(object)
    atomic_toggleoff_object(object)

# udp_cool_object(obj):
def udp_cool(object, loc):
    udp_pick_put_to(object, loc, fridge)


# udp_heat_object(obj):
def udp_heat(object, loc):
    udp_pick_put_to(object, loc, microwave)
    udp_toggle(microwave)
    udp_pick_up(object, microwave)

# udp_clean_object(obj):
def udp_clean(object, loc):
    udp_pick_put_to(object, loc, Faucet)
    udp_toggle(Faucet)
```

Table 11: Procedural functions defined by a programmer without ALFRED domain knowledge. The comments could roughly map to functions in Tab. 10.

Author Index

Association for Computational Linguistics
209 N. Eighth Street
Stroudsburg, Pennsylvania 18360

ISBN 978-1-7138-5642-9

CURRAN ASSOCIATES INC.
proceedings.com